Population Matters

ISSUES
(previously Issues for the Nineties)

Volume 20

Editor

Craig Donnellan

Independence
Educational Publishers
Cambridge

First published by Independence
PO Box 295
Cambridge CB1 3XP
England

British Library Cataloguing in Publication Data
Population Matters – (Issues Series)
I. Donnellan, Craig II. Series
304.6

ISBN 1 86168 044 9

Printed in Great Britain
City Print Ltd
Milton Keynes

Typeset by
Claire Boyd

Cover
The illustration on the front cover is by
Michaela Bloomfield.

CONTENTS

Introduction

Population Matters is the twentieth volume in the series: **Issues**. The aim of this series is to offer up-to-date information about important issues in our world.

Population Matters examines world population growth.

The information comes from a wide variety of sources and includes:
Government reports and statistics
Newspaper reports and features
Magazine articles and surveys
Literature from lobby groups
and charitable organisations.

It is hoped that, as you read about the many aspects of the issues explored in this book, you will critically evaluate the information presented. It is important that you decide whether you are being presented with facts or opinions. Does the writer give a biased or an unbiased report? If an opinion is being expressed, do you agree with the writer?

Population Matters offers a useful starting-point for those who need convenient access to information about the many issues involved. However, it is only a starting-point. At the back of the book is a list of organisations which you may want to contact for further information.

*****

Focus on population

In 1998 the world's population is likely to reach 6 billion. The last two decades have seen the fastest growth in world population ever recorded. It is currently increasing at a rate of 88 million people every year, the equivalent of 241,095 people a day, or 167 people a minute.

Trends

It took 123 years for world population to increase from 1 billion in 1804 to 2 billion in 1927. Succeeding billions have been reached in increasingly shorter periods of time. The next billion, taking the world's population to 6 billion, will have been reached in only 11 years.

The United Nations world population projection for 2015 ranges from a low of 7.1 billion people to a high of 7.8 billion. By the year 2050, the low projection is 7.8 billion people and the high projection 12.5 billion people. Even at the low level, world population would have tripled since 1950.

Population growth rates

The rate of population growth or decline is determined by the difference between the number of people being born and the number of people dying. This is usually expressed as a percentage. Europe currently has the lowest rate of population growth and Africa the highest.

If assistance is not given to enable couples to plan their families,

the effect on the world's population will be phenomenal. Providing women and men can obtain contraception if they require it, world population will probably level out at around 12 billion. Otherwise it is likely that it will triple to 17 billion over the next century.

There are many reasons for an increasing world population, including:

- a steep decline in the number of people dying (largely as a result of improvements in medicine and sanitation) has not been accompanied by a similar decline in the number of babies being born. However, this is beginning to change in many countries
- large families are still found in many regions of the world
- as world population has increased, so the total added to it has grown, as children grow up to have their own families
- a lack of access to family planning services of any kind.

The higher the rate of population growth in a developing

country, the harder it is for the government to meet the basic needs of the people, such as food and water. Access to education and health care, including family planning services, become more remote.

Current initiatives

Population control programmes aimed at meeting demographic targets have proved in the long term to be counter-productive. Most current programmes recognise that solving the population problem involves a mixture of projects covering education, gender equality, health care, sustainable economic development and family planning. In less economically developed countries (LEDCs) where fertility rates are stable or falling, the following factors have been identified as important:

- better status for women
- better provision for old age
- better education, especially for girls
- better education about birth control and better distribution of contraception.

The Cairo Population Conference

In 1994, an International Conference on Population and Development took place. Most governments recognise the need for slower population growth, but not all of them have the means or the education to do enough about it.

The Cairo Conference set out a 20-year programme to increase investment in women's reproductive health, including family planning services, and to combat sexually-transmitted diseases. The programme emphasises the importance of quality, the needs of men as well as women and the urgent help required by young people.

The challenges are to ensure that:

- everyone has access to reproductive health care and services
- men and women including young people are able to protect them-

The higher the rate of population growth in a developing country, the harder it is for the government to meet the basic needs of the people

selves against infection (most new HIV infections are among young people)

- children are conceived by choice
- women go through pregnancy and delivery more safely.

Some family planning success stories

In Mexico, where the majority of the population are Catholic, birth rates dropped by 20% in the decade after a national family planning programme was introduced.

In Nigeria, nearly 25% of new clients at family planning centres said that television shows giving clinic addresses prompted them to make their first visit.

In the Philippines a quarter of a sample of 600 young people aged between 15 and 25 said they sought contraceptive advice after seeing two music videos on family planning.

In Brazil, a vasectomy advertising campaign brought about a 54% increase in the number of vasectomies performed over the year.

• The above is an extract from *Global Eye*, published by Worldaware for the Overseas Development Administration. See page 41 for address details.

The state of world population 1997

- 585,000 women – one every minute – die each year from pregnancy-related causes, nearly all in developing countries. Many times this number are disabled as the result of childbirth. Much of this death and suffering could be averted with relatively low-cost improvements in health care systems.
- About 200,000 maternal deaths per year result from the lack or failure of contraceptive services.
- 120-150 million women who want to limit or space their pregnancies are still without the means to do so effectively. Altogether 350 million couples lack information about and access to a range of contraceptive services.
- At least 75 million pregnancies each year (out of about 175 million) are unwanted; they result in 45 million abortions, 20 million of which are unsafe.

- 70,000 women die each year as a result of unsafe abortion, and an unknown number suffer infection and other health consequences. Many unsafe abortions could be avoided if safe and effective means of contraception were freely available.
- 3.1 million people were infected last year by the human immuno-deficiency virus (HIV) which leads to AIDS; 1.5 million died from HIV/AIDS-related causes in 1996; 22.6 million people are living with HIV/AIDS.
- 1 million people die each year from reproductive tract infections including sexually transmitted diseases (STDs) other than HIV/AIDS. More than half of the 333 million new cases of STDs per year are among teenagers.
- 120 million women have undergone some form of female genital mutilation; another 2 million are at risk each year.

- Rape and other forms of sexual violence are rampant, though many rapes are unreported because of the stigma and trauma associated with rape and the lack of sympathetic treatment from legal systems.
- At least 60 million girls who would otherwise be expected to be alive are 'missing' from various populations as a result of sex-selective abortions or neglect.
- 2 million girls between ages 5 and 15 are introduced into the commercial sex market each year.

For further information:
Information and External Relations Division, United Nations Population Fund, 220 E. 42nd Street, New York, NY 10017, USA.

• The above is an extract from *The State of World Population 1997*.

Population to fall by 5m in 70 years

By David Brindle, Social Services Correspondent

The population of Britain will fall far more sharply than was previously thought and will be around 5 million less than now in 70 years' time, according to official projections.

The United Kingdom population is expected to peak in 2023 at more than 61 million, before falling to 54 million in 2061.

Government statisticians have revised their projections because they now think the birth rate will be even lower than estimated previously. As a result, they are expecting 2 million fewer births over the next 40 years.

The long-term assumption for the number of children born to each woman is now put at 1.8.

The new projections, by the Office for National Statistics, are based on the 1994 population figures. The last set was based on 1992 data. There were 58.4 million people in the UK in 1994, rising last year to 58.6 million. Numbers are projected to continue rising steadily to 59.5 million in 2001 and 61.1 million in 2021, before starting to fall at a rate accelerating to an annual net loss of 250,000 by the middle of the next century.

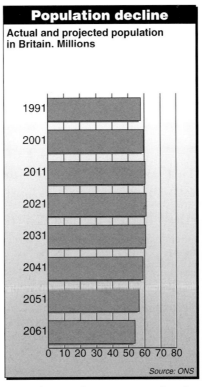

Population decline

Actual and projected population in Britain. Millions

Source: ONS

The new figures suggest that the population will be 1 million lower than previously projected by 2021, 2 million lower by 2039 and almost 4 million lower by 2064. The 2023 peak has also been brought forward by four years.

The lower official projections will have a marked impact on government planning for numbers of school places, health and welfare budgets and housing.

Numbers of under-16s are projected to fall by 574,000, or 5 per cent, by 2021 and by 829,000, or 7.3 per cent, by 2031.

In addition to a lower birth rate, the statisticians are also now expecting a slightly higher death rate than previously forecast among very elderly people. As a result, the ONS is projecting there will be 6 per cent fewer people over 75 by 2021 than it last suggested. This revision will effect forecasted expenditure on pensions and long-term social care.

Life expectancy is projected to rise from 74.2 years for men and 79.4 for women in 1994 to 79.0 for men and 83.9 for women in 2061. However, life expectancy for women in Japan is already 82.5 and UK figures are also below other European countries such as Sweden, Norway, Iceland, the Netherlands and Switzerland.

• National Population Projections, 1994-Based; Stationery Office; £23.50

© The Guardian
December, 1996

World population rises to 5·840 billion in 1997

By Carl Haub

The total number of the world's inhabitants rose to 5.840bn in mid-year 1997, according to the latest edition of the Population Reference Bureau's (PRB) *World Population Data Sheet*. Over the past 12 months, 86 million people were added to the global family, about 96 per cent of them in the world's less developed countries.

World-wide, women average 3.0 children each during their lifetimes, but this varies from an average of 1.6 in the more developed countries to 4.0 in the less developed countries excluding China. This figure, known as the total fertility rate, is more telling than any other of the demographic differences – and the very different potential for future population growth – between the world's rich and poor countries.

This year's *Data Sheet* features data on maternal mortality rates for most countries. Although information on maternal mortality is far from complete, we have clear evidence of the magnitude of these deaths around the world. The maternal mortality ratio is the number of deaths from causes related to pregnancy and childbirth per 100,000 live births. The ratio ranges from fewer than 5 in some European countries to more than 1,000 in some of the poorest countries in Africa.

> **PRB estimates that the world's annual rate of population growth is 1.47 per cent per year in 1997, down slightly from 1.52 per cent in 1996**

Maternal mortality ratios are highest in Africa, at nearly 900 maternal deaths per 100,000 live births, but vary greatly across the continent. The maternal mortality ratio for Botswana is estimated to be 250, and that for Namibia 370, while ratios are estimated to be at or above 1,500 for Angola, Chad, Guinea, Mozambique, Sierra Leone, and Somalia. In Asia, ratios are above 1,500 for Afghanistan, Bhutan, and Nepal, whereas the ratio for Japan is among the lowest at 9.

While maternal mortality in Latin America and the Caribbean is low for the developing world, about 180 deaths per 100,000 births, it is still 22 times that of neighbouring North America. In the United States, for each 100,000 babies born alive, eight women die of causes related to pregnancy and childbearing.

The main strategies for reducing maternal deaths include improving access to family planning services, community-based maternity care, and adequate emergency obstetric care. Recent declines in maternal mortality in some very poor countries show that dramatic reductions in death rates are possible in even the poorest countries.

Less developed countries home to four-fifths of world's people

PRB estimates that the world's annual rate of population growth is 1.47 per cent per year in 1997, down slightly from 1.52 per cent in 1996. This results in a 'doubling time' of 47 years, which means that world population would double if this growth rate remained unchanged.

World population clock 1997

	World	Developed Countries	Developing Countries	Developing Countries (less China)
Population	5,840,433,00	1,174,792,000	4,665,641,000	3,428,948,000
Births per:				
Year:	139,366,897	13,450,155	125,916,742	104,917,695
Month:	11,613,908	1,120,846	10,493,062	8,743,141
Week:	2,680,133	258,657	2,421,476	2,017,648
Day	381,827	36,850	344,977	287,446
Hour:	15,909	1,535	14,374	11,977
Minute:	265	26	240	200
Second:	4.4	0.4	4.0	3.3

Source: 1997 World Population Data Sheet, Population Reference Bureau, Inc

Population growth is expected to decline, but how fast depends on how quickly fertility declines in less developed countries. Currently, the world's less developed countries are home to 80 per cent of total world population, 4,665,641,000 people.

The population of the more developed countries stands at 1,174,792,000, barely more than last year. Europe continues to be the first major world region to experience natural decrease (more annual deaths than births) with a natural increase rate of -0.1 per cent. Europe's declining population reflects the recent inclusion of 10 states of the former Soviet Union in the European totals, along with sharp fertility declines in other eastern European states. The world's lowest fertility continues to be found in Italy and Spain, with total fertility rates of only 1.2 children per woman. And other countries, such as Bulgaria and the Czech Republic, now appear to be emulating this historic low birth rate.

The world's lowest fertility continues to be found in Italy and Spain, with total fertility rates of only 1.2 children per woman

The effect of AIDS on population growth has significant implications for the population of a number of African countries. New data collected by the US Bureau of the Census' International Programs Centre show higher prevalence levels than previously thought, resulting in lower population projections, particularly in countries such as Kenya and South Africa.

Another trend to watch carefully is the birth rate in India, where demographic targets were abandoned in 1996. Recent data on birth rates from the Registrar General's office show that the birth rate decline stalled from 1993 to 1994, pointing to the possibility of a slowdown in birth rate decline similar to that which occurred in India in the 1980s.

In this year's version of PRB's *Data Sheet*, Hong Kong is included with China since the former British colony became part of China on July 1, 1997 and the *Data Sheet* population reference date is mid-year. French Guinea is now printed on the wallchart because its population has reached more than 150,000.

• The Population Reference Bureau's 1997 *World Population Data Sheet* is available for $4.50 a copy, including shipping and handling. Data are available on diskette in Lotus, Excel or ASCII format. Price: $12.50. See page 41 for address details.

© Population Today
April, 1997

World population growing more slowly than expected

A United Nations survey has found that the world's population is growing more slowly in most places than expected a few years ago. It also found that the number of people being added to the world each year has begun to fall sooner than anticipated.

Analysts say that family planning and other aid programmes of the 1960s and 1970s that gave couples more control over the number of children they had, augmented by more recent moves to give women more economic power and social status, have paid off in steady, continuous fertility declines in every region.

But these gains could be reversed if foreign aid budgets continue to shrink.

The slowing rate of population

By Barbara Crossette in New York

growth can also be partly attributed to higher death rates in some areas, Joseph Chamie of the UN population division said. War and Aids have reduced life expectancy in Africa,

The figures, covering 1990 to 1995, show a population growth rate world-wide of 1.48 per cent a year, significantly lower than the 1.57 per cent projected

and it has also fallen in eastern Europe and the former Soviet Union.

The figures, covering 1990 to 1995, show a population growth rate world-wide of 1.48 per cent a year, significantly lower than the 1.57 per cent projected by a previous report in 1994. The world therefore contains 29 million fewer people than expected.

Fertility has declined over the same period to an average of 2.96 children per woman. The projected figure had been 3.1 children.

By 2050, UN analysts now say, the world's population could be 9.4 billion, nearly half a billion lower than 1994 projections. The current population is 5.77 billion – *New York Times*.

© The Guardian
November, 1996

Developing nations account for 98 per cent of world population growth

In 1997, the world's developing* countries accounted for 98 per cent of world population increase. The current prospect is for that imbalance to continue. This conclusion is drawn from the yearly report card of world population trends from the Population Reference Bureau (PRB), a Washington-based demographic research group. Data for all countries of the world appear on its annual *World Population Data Sheet*, a widely used source of global demographic trends.

World population now stands at 5.8 billion, 4.7 billion of whom live in the developing countries. By the century's end, world population will likely total 6.1 billion. And, by 2025, today's developing countries are projected to total about 6.8 billion while the developed countries remain at 1.2 billion, the same as today.

Given that world population amounted to just 1.6 billion in 1900, the nearly fourfold increase in the twentieth century led to the term 'population explosion'. But what of the next century? The *Data Sheet* offers some clues. For example, we can see that women in sub-Saharan Africa average about six children each during their lifetimes. While it is expected that birth rates will eventually decrease on that continent, it is difficult to predict just when or how fast that may happen.

World population amounted to just 1.6 billion in 1900, the nearly fourfold increase in the twentieth century led to the term 'population explosion'

Authoritative projections of world population size vary widely. Two major organisations produce different scenarios of world population projections, each using different assumptions about future trends in birth and death rates. United Nations projections for the year 2050 range from 7.7 to 11.2 billion by 2050. Similar projections from the International Institute for Applied Systems Analysis (IIASA) in Europe carry the scenarios further, to the year 2100. IIASA projections show an even wider range, from 4 to 23 billion for the more distant year 2100.

'The growth of global population is primarily concentrated in the world's poorest countries, that is clear,' said demographer Carl Haub. 'As a result, the future size of world population will be determined by the large number of developing countries with high and moderately high birth rates.

'New data from India, whose one billion inhabitants make it the second largest country in population after China, show that the decline in the birth rate may be stopped, a very serious concern to that country. India's population size by mid-century may rise to 1.2 billion and then slowly decline or it may be almost 2 billion and still growing. This is a perfect example of how statistically uncertain the future is.'

The use of family planning by many women in developing countries has been the key to prospects for slowing the growth of world population since WWII. 'But birth rates in developing countries apart from China remain at twice the level

needed to stabilise world population size at some point in the future,' he noted.

'The present demographic situation makes a large increase in numbers a mathematical certainty. That is something that we know. The great unknown is how large that increase will be,' said Haub. 'The outcome of this world concern is one of today's major stories.'

Other story tips from the Data Sheet

- The United States remains the world's industrialised country with the most population growth, adding 2.4 million people each year. About one-third of US growth results from immigration, the balance from natural increase, i.e. births minus deaths.

- AIDS remains a serious threat throughout sub-Saharan Africa whose effect on future population size is difficult to quantify. While it is not expected to cause the catastrophic population losses feared in the 1980s, Africa's population size in 2025 may be about 10 per cent less than it would have been without AIDS. In some countries in southern and eastern Africa, recent data show rising prevalence. Elsewhere,

---

The use of family planning by many women in developing countries has been the key to prospects for slowing the growth of world population since WWII

---

such as in Thailand, the epidemic may be stabilising.

- Extremely low birth rates continue throughout Europe and Japan. In Europe, this is thought to result from the effect of factors such as high unemployment and a high cost of living. There are at least two major stories here. First, Europe's populations are certain to age to the point where old-age support systems will be taxed beyond their limits. This altered age structure will likely lead to considerable modifications to the continent's well-known social 'safety net' programmes, a sure source of widespread labour unrest. Secondly, drastically reduced numbers of younger

---

Europeans will shrink markets, particularly among those of family formation ages. Europe also wonders where it will find its workers of the future.

- China's birth rate, brought down by a stringent government policy for smaller families, is a significant future unknown. It has now ceased its decline as a lifetime average of only about 1.8 children per woman, below that of the United States. The questions many demographers are asking: will it stay there? Or will a pent-up demand for more children cause an upsurge, perhaps in a climate of more liberal policies?

*The developing countries (also known as less developed), as defined by the United Nations, comprise the countries of Africa, Asia, Latin America, and Oceania, excluding Australia, Japan, and New Zealand.

• *The 1997 World Population Data Sheet*, prepared by PRB demographers Carl Haub and Diana Cornelius, is available free of charge to writers and members of the press. See page 41 for address details or e-mail your request to popref@prb.org

© *Population Reference Bureau May, 1997*

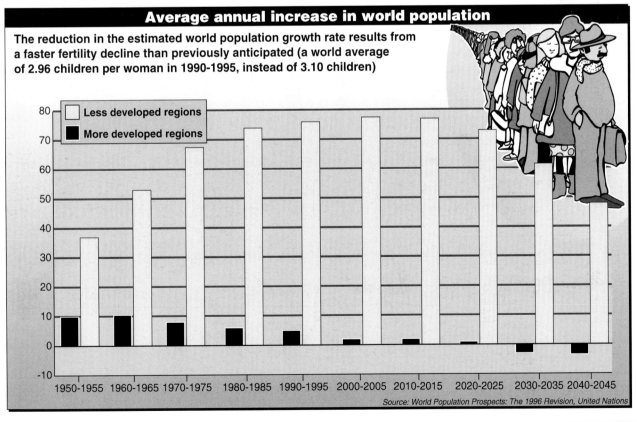

Average annual increase in world population

The reduction in the estimated world population growth rate results from a faster fertility decline than previously anticipated (a world average of 2.96 children per woman in 1990-1995, instead of 3.10 children)

Less developed regions
More developed regions

1950-1955 1960-1965 1970-1975 1980-1985 1990-1995 2000-2005 2010-2015 2020-2025 2030-2035 2040-2045

Source: World Population Prospects: The 1996 Revision, United Nations

Population growth and consumption

Environmentalists have long been concerned with human impact on the environment. Rapid population growth in developing countries and high levels of resource consumption in developed countries are considered to be important causes of environmental damage, but attempts to study the links between population and environment have demonstrated that the relationship is complex.

The following are significant environmental issues that have been linked to population growth and resource consumption on a global or regional scale.

Global warming

Most scientists now agree that a substantial proportion of the observed long-term rise in 'greenhouse gases' is due to human activity and that this rising concentration will increase world atmospheric temperatures. Uncertainties remain, however, about the magnitude of global warming and ensuing environmental impact. A projected rise in sea level of between 0.2 and 1 metre, for example, could have devastating effects on densely populated and low-lying Bangladesh, but have a negligible impact on landlocked countries. The health risks of higher temperatures, such as the spread of tropical diseases to new populations, would probably be greatest in subtropical areas. Climatic change, however, could also affect natural ecosystems in the northern latitudes.

Pollution

Population size, growth, and patterns of resource use can have an impact on all types of pollution, including air, water, and solid pollution. Pollutants are often concentrated in densely populated, urban areas. According to UN projections, by the

year 2005 the majority of the world's population will live in urban areas, where standards of living and consumption patterns often exceed those in rural areas. Labour availability, infrastructure, and transport facilities favouring industrial development can affect the severity of urban atmospheric and water pollution. Even in the absence of population growth, poor environmental policy and management can lead to serious environmental degradation. For example, despite its negative rate of population growth (-0.5 per cent), Russia faces significant environmental damage created by pollutants from the former Soviet Union's industries.

Ozone depletion

The most important causes of ozone depletion are consumption patterns and industry, not population growth. Slowing population growth is therefore unlikely to have much effect on the problem, but reducing or halting the industrial production of halocarbons (such as chlorofluorocarbons) can. The long-term impact of increased ultraviolet (UV) radiation on the Earth's organisms remains unclear. Studies continue to determine the impact of UV radiation on phytoplankton and krill, which are at the base of the marine food chain. A decline in these species could have catastrophic effects on

the world's food supply. Likewise, increases in UV radiation would also lead to higher incidences of skin cancer and cataracts, and cause damage to the human immune system.

Loss of biodiversity

The concept of biodiversity encompasses not only the number and diversity of plant and animal species, but the amount of variation within the same species. As human populations expand, they reduce biological diversity through the destruction of ecosystems such as tropical and temperate forests, tundra, wetlands, coral reefs, and marine environments. Diversity within species has also been an important factor, primarily in the development of agriculture and livestock. Historically, farmers have selected specimens that exhibit the 'most desired traits', leading to a narrowing of the genetic field of domesticated or cultivated species. In North America, for example, virtually all beef comes from only two breeds, and most milk from just one breed. Genetic uniformity raises the danger that crop and livestock resources could become more susceptible to diseases or pests, and that a small outbreak could become a regional or global epidemic.

Tropical forests

Population growth, and particularly migration, are clearly associated with the destruction of tropical forests. In addition to depleting a natural resource, deforestation is linked to loss of biodiversity, land degradation, and emission of greenhouse gases (where forests are burned). The migration of farmers in search of cultivable land, domestic and commercial export demands for tropical timber, the overcutting of wood fuel, and the indirect effects of clearing activities are all causes of deforestation. Studies show that rates of tropical deforestation in developing countries have been increasing since 1960.

Freshwater resources

Water is a renewable resource, but its rate of renewal depends on the global water cycle, which often cannot keep pace with human demands. Human impact on the flow and storage of fresh water, which makes up only 1 per cent of the world's water resources, has been growing significantly for centuries. Diversions, dams, irrigation works, and reservoirs have all affected the quality and quantity of fresh water available. The shrinking of the Aral Sea in Central Asia, for example, is a direct result of extensive irrigated cotton cultivation along two of its principal tributaries. Current patterns suggest that global demand for water for irrigation, household, and industrial use will increase faster than the rate of population growth.

Oceans and fisheries

Population growth, changing consumption patterns, and more efficient harvesting technologies have dramatically increased the demand on coastal and ocean resources world-wide. Rising populations along the world's coasts are intensifying pressures on coastal fisheries and wetlands, and at the same time pollution threatens to reduce the biological productivity of these areas. In the United States, 54 per cent of the population lives in counties adjacent to the coasts or surrounding the Great Lakes. Development along the coasts has directly affected the nation's wetlands, which are necessary for sustaining coastal fisheries, reservoirs, and filtering pollution.

Land use

Generalizations about the impact of population and land use must also consider the specific characteristics of local environments and socio-economic or political contexts. While population growth and density are important, in some cases society's institutions may be more important than the numbers. In Honduras, for

example, population impacts are secondary to social factors, such as land inequality and the investment patterns of large landowners, in exacerbating deforestation and soil erosion. In Zaire, where the urban population is growing more rapidly than the rural population, inappropriate use of tropical land resources to feed urban dwellers can result in erosion and reduced soil fertility. Likewise, cultivation on steeply inclined slopes in the Philippine uplands has dramatically increased erosion and land degradation. Topsoil loss from a single typhoon can leave the land unsuitable for cultivation and cause silt to build up in rivers downstream.

Carrying capacity

Human settlements, industry, and agriculture can all affect the Earth's carrying capacity – that is, the amount of life that the Earth can support. Recent estimates of the

---

Rapid population growth in developing countries and high levels of resource consumption in developed countries are considered to be important causes of environmental damage

---

Earth's carrying capacity range from fewer than 3 billion to more than 44 billion people, but while such global figures are often calculated, it is difficult to assess truly the Earth's capacity for human life. Estimates made at the local or regional level are considered more valid, but even these have considerable uncertainty.

The extent to which human settlement has changed the Earth's natural resource base is difficult if not impossible to quantify. It is none the less an area of great importance: changes in human behaviour and population size and distribution over time have all affected the environment in some way, either positively or negatively. As development efforts continue to better the lives of millions of people world-wide, environmentalists fear this action could threaten the environment to the point that 'human gains' are negated by environmental loss. In this decade, however, growing support for environmentally sustainable development is a positive sign that previously separate concerns for human development and environmental protection can be merged.

• This information, prepared by Kate Chalkley, is an updated summary of *Population and Consumption Issues for Environmentalists*, by Alex de Sherbinin (Washington, DC: Population Reference Bureau).

© *Population Today April, 1997*

Urban population dynamics

Urban dwellers will soon be a majority of the world's population. Not long after, they will be a majority in all regions of the world.

The percentage of people living in urban areas has increased dramatically during the past half century, particularly in the less-developed regions. The United Nations projects that a majority of the world population will be urban by 2005; in the less-developed regions, that threshold will be crossed before 2015. Of the world's 2.6 billion people currently living in urban areas, over 1.6 billion are in less-developed regions. These regions will include 3.2 billion out of 4.1 billion urban people world-wide in 2015, and over 4 billion out of 5.1 billion in 2025.

The urban population is increasing much faster in developing countries than in the more-developed regions.

In 1970, there were about as many city dwellers in developing countries as in the more-developed regions. The ratio is nearly two to one today; it will pass three to one by 2015 and approach four to one by 2025. Of the 1.23 billion urban residents added to the world population since 1970, 84 per cent have been in less-developed regions, and this proportion is growing. It is projected that less-developed regions will account for 92.9 per cent of a 2.06 billion increase in the global urban population between 1970 and 2020.

In terms of total population numbers, Asia now accounts for 1.2 billion of the 2.5 billion global urban residents (i.e. about 46 per cent). Europe accounts for 535 million more. By 2025, 23 new urban Asians will be added for every new European urban resident. Latin America and the Caribbean account for about 358 million current urban residents. In 2025, these numbers will be: Asia, 2.7 billion; Europe, 598 million; Latin America and the Caribbean, 601 million; and Africa, 804 million.

There is substantial variation in the level of urbanisation within regions. In Africa this ranges from 48 per cent in Southern Africa, 45 per cent in Northern Africa, 36 per cent in Western Africa and 33 per cent in Middle Africa to 21 per cent in Eastern Africa. These differences between African subregions result from historical patterns related to their governance and economic structures dating back to colonial times, and are expected to continue for at least the next 30 years. National levels range from 6.1 per cent in Rwanda to 85 per cent in the Libyan Arab Jamahiriya.

For Asian subregions the levels are: South Central Asia, 28.8 per cent; Eastern Asia, 36.9 per cent (the regional statistic is dominated by China's 30.0 per cent); and South-eastern Asia, 33.7 per cent. National levels vary from under 10 per cent in Bhutan to over 90 per cent in Hong Kong and Singapore. In Western

The 30 largest countries ranked according to population size

By the year 2050, India will become the most heavily populated country in the world.

	1996 Country	Population (million)		2050 Country	Population (million)
1	China	1,232	1	India	1,533
2	India	945	2	China	1,517
3	United States of America	269	3	Pakistan	357
4	Indonesia	200	4	United States of America	348
5	Brazil	161	5	Nigeria	339
6	Russian Federation	148	6	Indonesia	318
7	Pakistan	140	7	Brazil	243
8	Japan	125	8	Bangladesh	218
9	Bangladesh	218	9	Ethiopia	213
10	Nigeria	115	10	Iran (Islamic Republic of)	170
11	Mexico	93	11	Zaire	165
12	Germany	82	12	Mexico	154
13	Vietnam	75	13	Philippines	131
14	Iran (Islamic Republic of)	70	14	Vietnam	130
15	Philippines	69	15	Egypt	115
16	Egypt	63	16	Russian Federation	114
17	Turkey	62	17	Japan	110
18	Thailand	59	18	Turkey	98
19	France	58	19	South Africa	91
20	Ethiopia	58	20	United Republic of Tanzania	89
21	United Kingdom	58	21	Myanmar	81
22	Italy	57	22	Thailand	73
23	Ukraine	52	23	Germany	70
24	Zaire	47	24	Uganda	66
25	Myanmar	46	25	Kenya	66
26	Republic of Korea	45	26	Colombia	62
27	South Africa	42	27	Afghanistan	61
28	Spain	40	28	Yemen	61
29	Poland	39	29	Sudan	60
30	Colombia	36	30	Saudi Arabia	60

Source: Population Division, Department of Economic and Social Information and Policy Analysis of the United Nations Secretariat, World Population Proespects: The 1996 Revision, United Nations, New York, 1996

Asia, national levels vary from 13 per cent in Oman to over 90 per cent in Bahrain, Israel, Kuwait and Qatar.

Subregional urbanisation levels in Latin America and the Caribbean are 62.4 per cent in the Caribbean, 68 per cent in Central America and 78 per cent in South America. National levels range from 13.8 per cent in Montserrat, 31.6 per cent in Haiti and 41.5 per cent in Guatemala to 90.3 per cent in Uruguay and 100 per cent in the Cayman Islands and Bermuda.

Urban growth in less-developed regions is declining, but annual increments will continue to be very large into the next century.

The global urban population is growing by 2.5 per cent per year (3.5 per cent per year in the less-developed regions and 0.8 per cent in the more-developed regions), or 61 million people – roughly the equivalent of adding six cities the size of Lagos. Annual urban growth in the less-developed regions peaked at 5.1 per cent during 1955-1960. Today's rate of growth is slower because the base population is much larger, but the annual increments are greater. By the period 2020-2025 the global urban growth rate will have declined to under 2 per cent per year, but the urban population will increase by 93 million people – more than the current annual increase in the total world population.

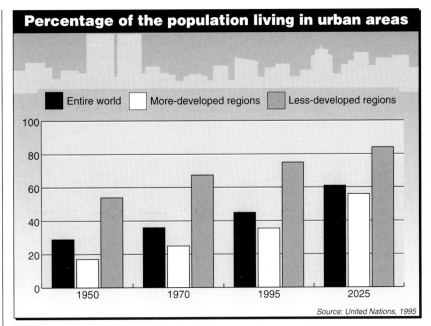

Percentage of the population living in urban areas

Entire world   More-developed regions   Less-developed regions

Source: United Nations, 1995

In 1970, there were about as many city dwellers in developing countries as in the more-developed regions. The ratio is nearly two to one today; it will pass three to one by 2015

The highest rate of urban growth is in Africa. Cities in Eastern Africa grew by more than 6 per cent a year between 1960 and 1980, reaching a high of 6.5 per cent during 1975-1980. A gradual decline to 4.1 per cent in 2020-2025 is anticipated. Southern Africa's urban growth rate, now 3.2 per cent, will decline to 2.3 per cent by 2020-2025.

Asia accounts for more than two-thirds of the annual increase in the global urban population. Within Asia, urban growth rates are more than 3.6 per cent per year in South-eastern Asia and Western Asia, compared to about 3 per cent in Eastern Asia (less if China is excluded). These subregions are expected to reach 2.2, 2.0 and 1.6 per cent urban growth, respectively, by 2020-2025.

© UNFPA
January, 1997

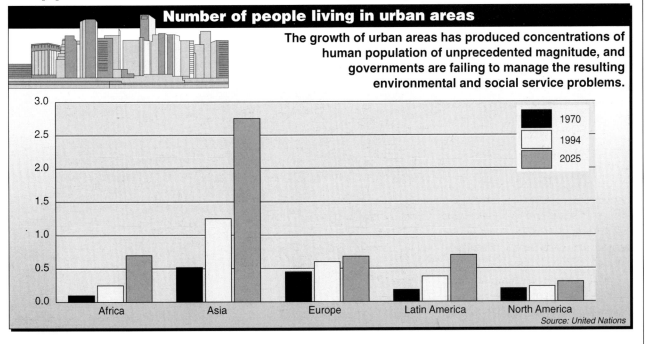

Number of people living in urban areas

The growth of urban areas has produced concentrations of human population of unprecedented magnitude, and governments are failing to manage the resulting environmental and social service problems.

1970
1994
2025

Africa   Asia   Europe   Latin America   North America

Source: United Nations

The processes of urban growth

Three different processes fuel urban population growth: natural growth (the excess of births over deaths), migration from rural areas, and cities' incorporation of rural surrounds (redefinition of administrative boundaries). The relative importance of each component changes as urbanisation proceeds.

When urbanisation levels are low (particularly when rural and urban fertility rates are similar), migration accounts for most of the growth difference between cities and rural areas. Natural increase becomes more important at higher levels of urbanisation. When economic opportunities in the cities expand rapidly, growth from migration may also increase.

Globally, natural increase accounts for nearly 60 per cent of urban growth. The contribution of rural urban migration differs significantly in different regions and over time.

By way of contrast, the rapid urban growth in Europe during the nineteenth century was largely attributable to migration, fuelled by the growing urban manufacturing sector. London's population more than doubled between 1801 and 1851. The 10 largest cities in England during this period increased from 16 to 23 per cent of the total national population. This was also a period of substantial migration to North America. It is estimated that if the population which left the United Kingdom had instead moved to its cities, urban growth would have exceeded 5 per cent a year. At this rate, the urban population would have doubled in 14 years, about the pace of urban growth observed in Africa since 1950.

The largest cities

City sizes and growth rates describe only part of the global transformation of where, and how, people live. The distribution of sizes of urban areas is changing dramatically. In 1950, only one city had a population of more than 10 million people. In 1994, there were 14 such cities, only four of which were in more-developed regions. By 2015 there will be 13 more, all in the less-developed regions.

The composition and distribution of the world's largest cities has changed dramatically over the past 45 years.

In 1950, only New York had a population exceeding 10 million. Eleven of the 15 largest cities were in more-developed regions. The 15th largest city, Berlin, had 3.3 million people. In 1970, three cities (Tokyo, New York and Shanghai) exceeded 10 million; seven of the top 15 were in less-developed regions, and the 15th largest had 6.7 million people.

By 1994, 14 of the top 15 cities had more than 10 million people. The largest, Tokyo, had reached 26.5 million (the only city with more than 20 million); 11 were in less-developed regions and the 15th largest city had 9.8 million. By 2015, seven cities will exceed 20 million (Tokyo will still be the largest, at 28.7 million); 13 of the top 15 will be in less-developed regions, and the 15th largest will have nearly 15 million.

Between now and 2010, Asia's share of the 15 largest urban agglomerations will grow from nine to 11, Africa's from zero to one. Latin America will go from having four of the 15 largest cities to two, and Northern America from two to one.

The growth rates of megacities have been changing over the past few decades and will continue to do so. The fastest growing megacities will be in the less-developed regions.

Megacities in the more-developed regions grew, on average, by less than 1 per cent per year between 1970 and 1990. Some, such as Los Angeles, Tokyo and Moscow, grew faster, while others, like New York, experienced negative growth.

In contrast, Bombay, Karachi, Lagos and Dhaka grew by 3.7, 4.7, 6.7 and 7.6 per cent, respectively,

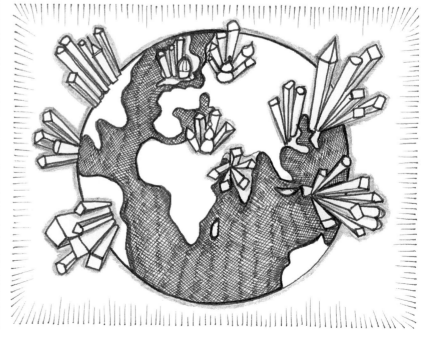

between 1970 and 1990. These growth rates will moderate before 2015. However, many of the cities projected to be megacities in 2015 will grow by more than 3 per cent per year between 1990 and 2000 (including Bangalore, Bombay, Dhaka, Delhi, Hyderabad, Istanbul, Jakarta, Karachi, Kinshasa, Lagos, Lahore and Metro Manila).

Six megacities are projected to grow faster than 3 per cent per year during 2000-2015: Dhaka, Hyderabad, Karachi, Lagos, Lahore and Kinshasa. Dhaka's 2015 population is projected to be more than 13 times larger than its 1970 population; Lagos's will be over 11 times larger. Slower growth rates are expected in Istanbul, Lima, Mexico City, São Paulo and Seoul.

The proportion of the population living in the largest cities is increasing.

In 1990, 7.5 per cent of the urban population in more-developed regions was concentrated in the four cities with more than 10 million people; by 2015, these four cities will account for about the same share of the urban total, 7.2 per cent. In the less-developed regions, however, the change will be dramatic: from 98 million people (6.9 per cent of the total urban population) in eight cities of over 10 million in 1990 to 378 million (12.0 per cent) in 23 such cities by 2015.

At the same time, substantial change is expected in the distribution of cities of smaller sizes, particularly in the less-developed regions. The number of cities of 5-10 million people will increase from 15 to 36 between 1990 and 2015, and the population in them will more than double (from 110 million to 226 million), even as the proportion of the urban population in this size class declines slightly. Cities in the range of 1-5 million people will increase from 151 to 352, with their combined populations increasing from 283 to 701 million. Both the number and population of those in the 500,000 to 1 million range will increase by about 50 per cent.

Cities of fewer than 500,000 people will continue to account for more than half of the urban population at least through 2015. Those

In the more-developed regions, the greatest growth in numbers and population will occur in cities of 1-5 million people

in the less-developed regions will contain more than twice as many people in 2015 than in 1990 (1.64 billion compared to 812 million), though their share of the urban total will decrease slightly. In the more-developed regions, the greatest growth in population will occur in cities of 1-5 million people.

Regional patterns of city size distribution and growth vary substantially. In Africa, the proportion of people living in urban areas grew from 14.7 per cent in 1950 to 34 per cent in 1994. In 1950, 80 per cent of the urban population lived in cities of fewer than 500,000 people; this proportion declined to 60 per cent by 1994 and is expected to fall to 54 per cent by 2015. Africans are becoming increasingly concentrated in larger urban areas. Nearly 19 per cent will live in cities with over 5 million inhabitants by 2015, compared to 8.1 per cent in 1994.

In Asia, the number of cities in each of the size classes over 1 million people will more than double between 1990 and 2015. The greatest proportional growth will occur in cities of over 10 million.

Latin America and the Caribbean is the only less-developed region where cities of 500,000 to 1 million will contain a majority of the urban population by 2015. Cities of 1-5 million will show the largest growth, increasing from 32 to 69 in number, from 61 to 132 million in population, and from 19.4 to 25.2 per cent in their share of the total urban population.

Europe over the next quarter century will see little change in either the numbers of cities or the total populations in the various size groups; nearly two-thirds of the population will continue to reside in cities of under 500,000.

In Northern America, the proportional distribution of population among city sizes will change little between 1990 and 2015. Unlike Europe, less than 40 per cent of the urban population is in smaller cities. Oceania's urban population pattern, dominated by Australia and New Zealand, is not expected to change.

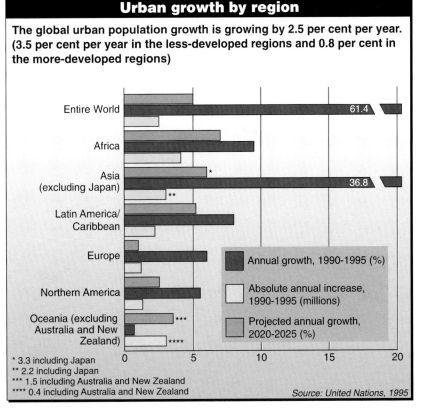

Urban growth by region

The global urban population growth is growing by 2.5 per cent per year. (3.5 per cent per year in the less-developed regions and 0.8 per cent in the more-developed regions)

Entire World — 61.4
Africa
Asia (excluding Japan) * — 36.8
  **
Latin America/ Caribbean
Europe
Northern America
Oceania (excluding Australia and New Zealand) *** / ****

Annual growth, 1990-1995 (%)
Absolute annual increase, 1990-1995 (millions)
Projected annual growth, 2020-2025 (%)

0   5   10   15   20

* 3.3 including Japan
** 2.2 including Japan
*** 1.5 including Australia and New Zealand
**** 0.4 including Australia and New Zealand

Source: United Nations, 1995

Harried by the mob

**Lucy Hodges reports on the challenges facing a world
with six billion inhabitants**

The statistics are sobering. Global population, which stands at 5.7 billion, is expected almost to double by the middle of the next century. It took until 1804 for the world to breed one billion people; by 1974 we reached four billion; the fifth billion came in 1987; and the sixth will arrive shortly.

But how much does rapid population growth matter, and what should be done about it? For biologists and family planning experts, for example, population growth is a critical issue. 'It is perhaps one of the greatest problems facing humankind at the moment,' says Mark Laskin, assistant secretary general of the International Planned Parenthood Federation. For economists such as the American Julian Simon of the University of Maryland it does not matter because humans are innovative and, given market mechanisms, will find ways to deal with shortages of resources.

Many academics regard population growth as important largely as it interferes with the development of poor countries and others see it primarily as a problem for women, inasmuch as repeated pregnancies are a drain on women's health, labour and time.

The bulk of the increase is in the Third World, where resources are already stretched. Figures from the World Bank illustrate the problem dramatically. Between 1970 and 1985 the estimated proportion of the Third World's population in absolute poverty dropped from 52 per cent to 44 per cent. That decline was cause for celebration. But closer examination of the figures shows that the number of people living in absolute poverty in the world actually increased over the period by 212 million.

A more tendentious area for debate is the environment – the extent to which global warming and acid rain are linked to population growth. Everyone is agreed that the so-called global commons, the air and the oceans and the Amazon rainforest, are under pressure and that an ever-expanding population cannot help but put pressure on such resources. But what should be done? In the 1970s when the world woke up to the issue after publication of biologist Paul Erlich's book, *The Population Bomb*, the West began pouring money into family planning campaigns in the Third World. Some governments, notably those of China and India, ran programmes to force women to accept sterilisation and birth control.

Since then there has been a backlash by feminists and by people in the Third World. 'There is a feeling in many developing countries that they do not want to have their policies dictated by developed

countries,' says Tom Gabriel, director of the Sir David Owen Population Centre at the University of Wales, Cardiff. The United Nations conference on population in Cairo in 1994 reflected that mood and put the emphasis squarely on individual rights to contraception rather than on imposing top-down targets.

Clearly, contraception would come in handy. There are large numbers of abortions; in some Latin American countries, for example, abortion is the main single cause of adult female mortality. But many of the experts argue that contraception is only one of a number of solutions to limiting population growth. Others are a reduction in child mortality – improving child health so that people do not feel the need to have such big families – and education.

World Bank figures show that girls who go to school turn into women who desire fewer children than their own mothers. Women with more than seven years of education tend to marry later than women with no education, with consequent delays in childbearing.

One or two people argue that contraception is almost irrelevant. For doctrinal reasons the Catholic Church is against what it calls artificial contraception, putting its faith instead in 'natural' birth control. And World Bank economist Lant Pritchett says that all fertility decline is explained by lower desired fertility, not by availability of contraception.

If nothing is done to check the growth in the world's population, the suggestion is that the gap between haves and have-nots will widen, cities will face extreme pressures, because almost all developing country growth will be urban, and rapid urbanisation will contribute to pollution.

Is population growth in the Third World a problem? If so, how should we deal with it?

'Every baby, and every additional person, is a problem. Every parent knows that. But the baby is not just a problem. It is also a source of benefits. That's true of every investment. Getting a house is a problem, getting it built is an investment, but eventually it brings benefits. In the long run, human beings are the source of all our benefits. The problem with an awful lot of this is simply bad thinking. On balance people create a little more than they use over their lifetimes.

'Population economics is uncommonsensical in the extreme. The most important effects of population growth are very diffuse and very hard to see. All the benefits are hard to see, whereas all the bad things are obvious. Which is why again and again we get all these stories presenting the view that population growth is all bad.'

Julian Simon, Economist, University of Maryland, United States

'I think the environment issue is the one reason why Western countries should be concerned about population growth in the Third World. The more people there are in newly industrialising countries, the more consumers there will be in the year 2050, presumably consuming at pretty close to the level that we are currently consuming, which is actually impossible. Massive changes in technology will be needed to accommodate that. And if we can keep the total towards the lower end, then our task will be easier.

'But it's important that the environmental concern should never be used as an excuse for hasty programmes, nor programmes that violate women's rights. The Chinese are very definitely violating women's rights. Family planning programmes ought to be set out with a perspective of helping women improve their choices. They should not set out with any other perspective such as reducing population numbers.'

Paul Harrison, Population and environment consultant

'I would say without doubt it is a problem. You have to deal with it on several different layers. We are all referring to rapid population growth in poor countries under conditions of high fertility. The more siblings a child has the more likely he is to be malnourished, the more likely he is to die young, and the less likely he, or particularly she, is to go to school. The large family is not good for children. Even with the parents, it's not all clear, especially when you add that the wife is more likely to die. In Africa mothers have one chance in six of dying as a result of having a child.

'We don't know whether rapid population growth in poor countries is good or bad for economic growth.

There's quite a lot of concern on the environmental score. People have been pointing out for years that it's the rich countries where population isn't growing that have been destroying the environment more than poor countries, which is true. But that doesn't mean to say it's not a problem in developing countries. India is already the world's fifth or sixth largest emitter of greenhouse gases.'

Robert Cassen, Oxford University

'Yes, I think it's a problem. I don't think it is for us to deal with it because unless the motivation to limit families comes from the individuals themselves, things that we do won't particularly help.

'I think the environment problems are overstated. A much more serious problem is that you can't keep up with the human resources you need to develop the population.

'If the population is growing at 3 per cent a year, you need 3 per cent more teachers each year – double the number of teachers every 17 years.

'If you want actually to increase the level of education of your population you've really got an uphill struggle. This is where population growth makes it very difficult for a country to develop.'

Basia Zaba, Senior lecturer, Centre for Population Studies, London School of Hygiene and Tropical Medicine

'It's a problem, but not the problem which many people allege. Clearly many governments in the Third World do perceive population growth as a serious problem and the extreme example is China with its strong government programme and the coercive practices that have gone on there.

'At the Cairo conference there was a strong emphasis on reproductive choice: the rights and needs of individual people, rather than governments, to control population. So often programmes which have clear targets to reduce fertility to a particular level spill over into coercive practices. The emphasis is on the right for everyone, especially women, to have access to the information and the means to have as many children as they wish.'

John Hobcraft, LSE, one of the lead negotiators for the United Kingdom at the Cairo Population Conference 1994

'The North really concentrates on population because it wants to apportion blame to the Third World. In fact 20 per cent of the population living in the North consumes 80 per cent of the world's resources. So, I would say population is not the only problem: the other is the distribution of the world's resources.

'We would not promote any programme that involved artificial contraception but that doesn't mean we are opposed to family planning. There are some benefits to natural family planning because it's not altering women's hormonal make-up. CAFOD is completely opposed to any kind of coercion. There are so many basic rights that women don't have – education, access to water. The North keeps pushing this one solution – curbing population growth – and it's not the answer.'

Linda Jones, Campaign co-ordinator, public education, Catholic Fund for Overseas Development (CAFOD)

Good news for 2050

There may be good news on the population front in years to come

The world's population in 2050 is expected to be 9.4 billion, according to the new UN medium population projection. This is good news: it is a massive 466 million less than the last projection done in 1994 – and 652 million less than the long-range projection made in 1992, writes Paul Harrison.

The annual increase for the 1990s is still high – an average of 81 million each year. But it is nearly a Switzerland a year less than the 87 million estimated in 1994, and a Netherlands a year less than the 97 million estimated in 1992.

The main reason for the changes is that childbearing has fallen faster than previously expected in many countries – and fallen lower than expected in developed countries. The typical lifetime number of children per woman in developed countries in 1995-2000 is 1.59 – 6.5 per cent less than expected in the 1994 projection, and well below the 2.1 necessary for replacement. For developing countries the total fertility rate is 3.1 – 11.5 per cent lower than expected in 1994.

Almost all regions are projected to have lower populations than the 1994 projection expected. The biggest differences are in South Asia, where the 2050 population is expected to total 2,521 million (152 million less than in the 1994 projection). Here India and Bangladesh have both seen fertility fall much faster than expected – it currently stands at around 3.1 for both countries. The global low population projection for 2050 is now 7.66 billion (255 million less than in the 1994 projection) and the high projection 11.2 billion (756 million less than expected in 1994).

So far, the long-term record of UN population projections has been remarkably good. That may not remain so in the future. It is quite possible that future projections will continue to lower the totals expected for 2050. The reason is that the medium projection assumes that fertility will not drop below the replacement level of 2.1 in countries where it is now above that level. In countries where fertility is below 2.1, the medium projection assumes that it will rise again back to 2.1. This assumption has a bigger and bigger effect on projected totals as the years advance. By the year 2025, most countries outside Africa are clocked in at an unchanging fertility rate of 2.1, right up to 2050, or rising towards 2.1. These figures are no longer projections, but assumptions. Events will almost certainly prove them wrong.

For example, all countries in Eastern Asia, except Mongolia, are now at or below replacement level.

Childbearing has fallen faster than previously expected in many countries

---

Here the medium projection expects fertility to rise from an average of 1.78 in 1995-2000, to 2.1 by 2040-45. All European countries except Malta, Albania and Iceland are below replacement fertility, often far below, but the average fertility is assumed to rise from 1.45 now to 2.03 in 2045-2050.

Yet many trends in both these regions are pushing to lower fertility, while few are pushing to raise it. Individualistic consumption is growing, urbanisation is increasing housing shortages and congestion, and women are delaying marriage and childbearing in favour of work and more education.

If fertility does not stick at replacement level, then the 2050 totals will be lower than is now expected – possibly as much as 450 million lower for East Asia and Europe alone. There may be more good news on the population front in years to come.

• This article was reproduced from *People and the Planet*. For subscription contact 1 Woburn Walk, London, WC1H 0JJ. Tel: 0171 383 4388.

© *People and the Planet*
Vol. 6, 1997

What population problem?

Information from the Alan Guttmacher Institute

The debate over whether there is such a condition as overpopulation and, if so, what it means and what to do about it may continue for decades to come. It is clear, however, that dilemmas involving population issues confront virtually all nations. Depending on the country, these might include high rates of teenage and unintended pregnancy, migration across national borders, urbanisation, an ageing population (in industrialised countries) and the youth bulge (in the developing world). These, among other factors, affect a key determinant of the quality of life: the balance between population growth and economic development.

Indeed, it is just such a balance that countries are striving to achieve. The ICPD's Programme of Action summarises the issue this way:

'Efforts to slow down population growth, to reduce poverty; to achieve economic progress, to improve environmental protection, and to reduce unsustainable consumption and production patterns are mutually reinforcing. Slower population growth has in many countries bought more time to adjust to future population increases.'

The disconcerting fact is that the world's current population of almost six billion is growing by 81 million people each year (equivalent to about one-third the population of the United States), but economic development and the availability of renewable natural resources are not keeping pace with this growth. In addition, after years of rapid population growth, a record number of people are about to enter the child-bearing years. Thirty-five per cent of the population in the developing world is under the age of 15 (as opposed to 20% in the developed world); in Sub-Saharan Africa, about

half of the population is younger than 15. This means that even if all couples were to have only two children (enough to replace themselves), the world's population would continue growing for many years to come because of the large absolute number of people having children. The world's population is expected to increase by 319 million people by the turn of the century.

The 'population problem' also can be defined in terms of women's self-described 'unmet need' for high-quality family planning services. An estimated 230 million women worldwide do not have access to effective contraceptive methods and services, representing approximately one in six women through the developing world. The reasons for this unmet need include a lack of accurate information, poor-quality services and less than the full range of contraceptive choices, as well as

legal, cultural and economic obstacles.

A compelling indicator of the failure to help women meet their childbearing goals is the 52 million abortions – half of them illegal – that occur world-wide each year, according to the World Health Organisation. Another is the large number of pregnancies that women report ending as unwanted or mistimed births: about 60% in Kenya; 50% in Japan, Mexico and the Philippines; and 40% in Egypt, Jordan and the United States.

These indicators of a population problem do have solutions. Making abortion less necessary can be achieved in large part through greater access to preventive family planning services. And that, in turn, could be expected to significantly lower the staggering number of maternal deaths that occur each year in connection with pregnancy and childbirth.

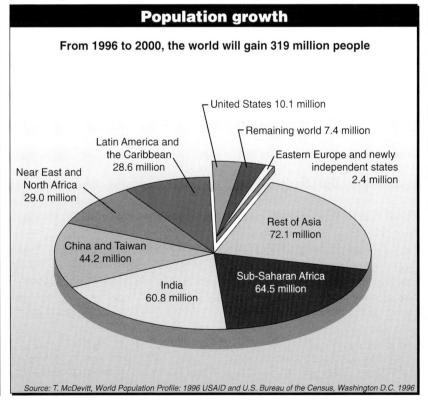

Population growth

From 1996 to 2000, the world will gain 319 million people

- United States 10.1 million
- Remaining world 7.4 million
- Eastern Europe and newly independent states 2.4 million
- Latin America and the Caribbean 28.6 million
- Near East and North Africa 29.0 million
- Rest of Asia 72.1 million
- China and Taiwan 44.2 million
- Sub-Saharan Africa 64.5 million
- India 60.8 million

Source: T. McDevitt, World Population Profile: 1996 USAID and U.S. Bureau of the Census, Washington D.C. 1996

In addition, reducing the rate of unintended pregnancy, and therefore improving women's ability to achieve their own childbearing goals, would not only benefit the lives of individuals, but also have a significant impact globally. If all unwanted births were prevented, the annual number of births world-wide would drop from 130 million to 122 million – a decline of almost 19% in the global rate of population.

Is progress possible?

In light of the seemingly overwhelming size and scope of the population problem, ameliorating the situation may appear impossible. There are encouraging signs, however. The United Nations' recent announcement that the planet is growing by 81 million people annually may sound daunting, but the fact that it is only 81 million more people each year means that global population growth already is slowing down.

Between 1985 and 1990, which was the peak period of population growth in human history, the world's population grew by 87 million people annually. The decline in the growth rate that has been observed more recently has been attributed to the introduction of programmes in the 1960s and 1970s that enabled people to begin to have the smaller families they wanted by increasing access to family planning services. More recent efforts to enhance women's economic power and social status have also played a key role.

The drop in the population growth rate to about 1.5% per year (from 2.5% in the 1960s) largely reflects a decrease in the average number of children each woman is having. Over the last 30 years, average family size in developing countries has dropped from 6.0 children to 3.3. This phenomenon also corresponds to improvements in related health and social in-dicators, such as lower infant mortality rates and improved female literacy. Together, these results suggest that at both the global and the individual levels, there has been enormous progress.

Over the same period, developing countries gradually have begun to adopt formal policies addressing the issue of population growth. Of the 125 developing countries that participated in the ICPD, more than half reported that they already have policies in place. Further, virtually all developing countries subsidise family planning programmes, even if they have not yet adopted a formal policy. The combination of financial and technical resources, political commitment, and laws and policies that protect and respect the rights and conscience of the individual and promote personal health and well-being are equally key to the success that world-wide efforts have seen so far.

© Alan Guttmacher Institute

Young people and the world

Information from the International Planned Parenthood Federation

There are over 1.5 billion people between the ages of 10 and 24, 85% of them living in developing countries. Young people in this age group make up 29% of the total population in developing countries but only 21% in developed countries. By 2025, there are expected to be almost 2 billion people in this age group.

Puberty occurs earlier and the average age at marriage is rising. This means that young people today face a longer period of time during which they are sexually mature and may be sexually active, but sexual activity and pregnancy may be neither desired nor socially acceptable.

In Sub-Saharan Africa 8 out of 10 young people below the age of 20 are sexually experienced, as are 7 out of 10 teenagers in many developed countries and at least half of all teens in Latin America.

Pregnancy and parenthood

One in every 10 births world-wide is to teenage mothers, In the least developed countries, 1 in every 6 births is to young women aged 15-19. In West Africa and South Asia, around 50% of young women have a child by age 20, as do one-third of young women in Latin America. Early pregnancy (before age 18) carries many health risks: girls aged 10-14 are 5 times more likely to die in pregnancy or childbirth than women aged 20-24.

Sexually transmitted diseases (STDs) and HIV/AIDS

Around half a million young people are infected with an STD every day. Every year, 1 in 20 teenagers becomes infected with an STD. Young adults in the 20-24 years age group are most likely to contract an STD, followed by those in the 15-19 years age group.

Young people under age 25 account for half of all HIV infections. Every day at least 4,000 people under age 25 are infected with HIV, predominantly in South-East Asia and sub-Saharan Africa.

Abortion

At least 1 in 10 abortions world-wide occurs among women aged 15-19. As many as 5 million young women have abortions every year, 40% of which are performed under unsafe conditions.

• The above is an extract from *Generation 97*, produced jointly by the International Planned Parenthood Federation (IPPF) and the United Nations Population Fund (UNFPA).

© *International Planned Parenthood Federation (IPPF), United Nations Population Fund (UNFPA)*

15m babies are born world-wide to adolescents each year

Young women less likely than their mothers' generation to have babies by age 20

New York, NY, USA (February 13, 1997) – one in five people in the world are adolescents (between the ages of 10 and 19) – the largest generation of youth in history. The sheer size of this vital segment of the world's population commands attention: They number nearly 1.1 billion – 913 million in developing countries and 160 million in developed countries – according to a new analysis by the Alan Guttmacher Institute (AGI), *Risks and Realities of Early Childbearing Worldwide.*

Far fewer women today are becoming mothers before age 20 – most notably in Asia. North Africa, the Middle East and parts of Latin America. None the less, in most countries in Sub-Saharan Africa, five or six of every 10 young women have a child during their adolescence, and in many Latin American countries, one-third of young women do so. While adolescents account for slightly more than 10% of all births world-wide – about 15 million each year – a high proportion of these births are not planned or not wanted.

Among other advantages, delaying childbearing until after age 20 has significant health benefits for mother and baby: the risk of death during childbirth is two to four times higher among women aged 17 and younger than among women 20 and older; the risk of dying in the first year of life is typically greater by 30% or more among babies whose mothers are aged 15-19 than among those aged 20-29.

Jeannie Rosoff, president of AGI, a nonprofit research organisation, says: 'We see encouraging signs that young women are now more likely to delay childbearing. Although this progress is uneven, much change has taken place in a short time period indicating enormous potential for swifter change if more is done to support adolescents in their life-altering decisions. Young people everywhere – in particular, young girls – need more and better schooling and job opportunities. They need and deserve more support from their families and communities in making the decisions that are right for them about when and if to have a child. They need better access to family planning and reproductive health services to help them achieve these goals. Even the poorest countries can do much by

---

Far fewer women today are becoming mothers before age 20 – most notably in Asia, North Africa, the Middle East and parts of Latin America

---

adopting sound policies, but the richer, more developed countries must help, too. US international population assistance, which has contributed so much to the progress we observe, must continue. Our global future is at stake.'

The Institute's new comprehensive, comparative examination of the extent to which adolescents around the world are becoming parents – and the social, economic and health-related consequences of early childbearing – includes information on adolescents in 44 developing and five developed countries, covering 75% of the world's total population. It reveals that the world has made great strides in the last few decades in raising education levels for young women but that they still lag behind those of young men in many countries. Significant advances have also been made in delaying marriage and childbearing, but in some areas of the world, these events still take place in early adolescence.

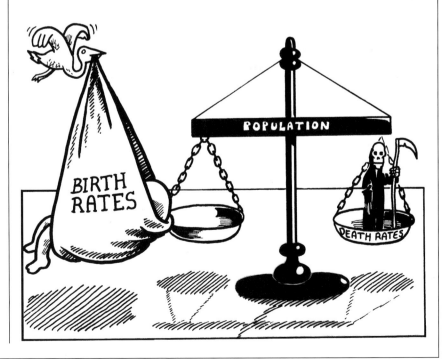

Number of births to youth still high; a significant proportion are unplanned

Despite the progress over the past 20 years, it is still common for young women to have their first child during their adolescent years.

- Roughly 35% of young women in Latin America and the Caribbean have their first child before they turn 20.
- 50-60% of young women in Sub-Saharan Africa have their first child before the age of 20; in Niger, this is true for 75% of young women.
- In the United States, 19% of all young women give birth before they turn 20; the United States has the highest levels of adolescent childbearing among developed countries – nearly three times the level of France, and nine times as high as Japan.

Education helps delay childbearing, but many girls are sill poorly educated

Another striking – and encouraging – finding of the analysis is the connection between delayed child-

---

50-60% of young women in Sub-Saharan Africa have their first child before the age of 20

---

bearing and higher levels of girls' education. Overall, young women with at least seven years of schooling are two to three times more likely than young women with less schooling to postpone having a baby until after age 20.

- In Colombia, 46% of young women with less than seven years of schooling have their first baby by age 20, compared with 19% of those with more education.
- In Egypt, 51% of less educated young women have their first birth before age 20, compared with 9% of those who are better educated.
- In the United States, 58% of young women who do not complete 12 years of school give birth by age 20, compared with 13% of

---

young women who complete at least 12 years of schooling.

- In France, 28% of less educated women have their first child by 20, compared with 3% of young women who have more than seven years of schooling.

But, while young women are better educated today than women 20 years ago, in many countries a high proportion only have some primary schooling or have not attended school at all – and they still lag far behind their male counterparts.

And a high proportion of births to adolescents are either earlier than they wished or not wanted at all.

- In 11 of the 20 Sub-Saharan African countries studied, one-third or more births to adolescents are unplanned; in Botswana, a striking case, 71% of the births to women aged 15-19 are un-planned.
- The level is the same – one-third or more – for seven of the 10 Latin American countries studied; in Brazil, half the births to adolescents are unplanned.

© *The Alan Guttmacher Institute*
February, 1997

Scientists warn of ageing population next century

By the end of the twenty-first century, four out of 10 people could be over 60, scientists say today. The world population would probably not double in that time, but populations would age dramatically as families got smaller.

Wolfgang Lutz, of the International Institute for Applied Systems Analysis, and colleagues in New York and the Netherlands report in *Nature* on the latest population projections.

Guessing what people will do a few decades from now is difficult, and what makes it more difficult is that forecasters inevitably tend to change the picture of the future they are trying to forecast.

By Tim Radford, Science Editor

Between 2030 and 2050, the scientists think, fertility rates will have fallen. Women in Africa would have between two and four children each; women in China and India would have between 1.5 and three children each. Populations would

---

In Europe in 2050, on the worst assumption, 43 per cent of the population would be over 60

---

grow dramatically in the Middle East, Sub-Saharan Africa and North Africa – they could quadruple by 2100.

Populations in eastern Europe and the former Soviet Union, however, were likely to fall. In Europe and the Pacific countries, the population was likely to be stable.

A falling fertility rate and better health care meant that the proportion of the population which was old would increase. In Europe in 2050, on the worst assumption, 43 per cent of the population would be over 60, although the best guess was 35 per cent. The 'youngest' region would be Sub-Saharan Africa.

© *The Guardian*
June, 1997

Reproductive neglect violates human rights

Gaps and failures in reproductive healthcare, combined with widespread discrimination and violence against women, amount to a massive violation of human rights, states the State of World Population Report 1997

The UNFPA report says the denial of sexual and reproductive rights – including free choice with regard to pregnancy and childbearing – causes millions of deaths every year, and much more illness and disability. Most of those affected are women, the vast majority in developing countries.

The report, titled *The Right to Choose: Reproductive Rights and Reproductive Health*, stresses the need for gender equality and increased investment in education and primary healthcare so that individuals can exercise their sexual and reproductive rights which the report states 'are key to women's empowerment and are also critical to the economic and social life of communities, nations and the world'.

The State of World Population 1997 documents the effects of the denial of these sexual and reproductive rights to millions of men and women:

It states: 'Global and national needs coincide with personal rights and interests. Given the choice, most women would have fewer children than their parents' generation. Ensuring that women and their partners have the right to choose will support a global trend towards smaller families, and help countries find a balance between their populations and resources.

'Successful development efforts will in turn bring sexual and reproductive health to more people.'

• 585,000 women – one every minute – die each year from pregnancy-related causes, nearly all in developing countries.

• 120-150 million women who want to limit or space their pregnancies are still without the means to do so effectively. Altogether 350 million couples lack information about and access to a range of contraceptive services.

• At least 75 million pregnancies each year (out of about 175 million) are unwanted; they result in 45 million abortions, 20 million of which are unsafe.

• 70,000 women die each year as a result of unsafe abortion, and an unknown number suffer infection and other health consequences.

Many unsafe abortions could be avoided if safe and effective means of contraception were freely available.

• One million people die each year from reproductive tract infections including sexually transmitted diseases (STDs) other than HIV/AIDS. More than half of the 333 million new cases of STDs each year are among teenagers.

• 3.1 million people were infected last year by the human immunodeficiency virus (HIV) which leads to AIDS; 1.5 million died from HIV/AIDS-related causes in 1996; 22.6 million people are living with HIV/AIDS.

© *Population Concern News 1997*

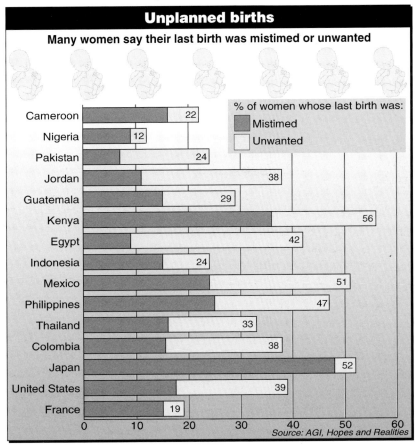

Unplanned births

Many women say their last birth was mistimed or unwanted

% of women whose last birth was:
- Mistimed
- Unwanted

Country	Value
Cameroon	22
Nigeria	12
Pakistan	24
Jordan	38
Guatemala	29
Kenya	56
Egypt	42
Indonesia	24
Mexico	51
Philippines	47
Thailand	33
Colombia	38
Japan	52
United States	39
France	19

Source: AGI, Hopes and Realities

Several countries advancing women's rights

By Wendy Shapiro

Reproductive rights are finally moving to the forefront of the international agenda, a recent report by the Center for Reproductive Law and Policy assures us.

Pledges made at six recent international conferences demonstrate long overdue concern for issues associated with advancing women's human rights. More importantly, several countries appear to be following through on these pledges.

For example, US Secretary of State Madeline Albright instructed American embassies abroad to consider advancement of women's rights as an integral foreign policy objective. She stressed that advancing the status of women is 'our mission, the right thing to do, and frankly it is the smart thing to do'.

Reed Boland's report, *Promoting Reproductive Rights: A Global Mandate*, outlines how each major international conference in this decade focused on issues connected to women's rights:

- The 1992 United Nations Conference on Environment and Development held in Rio de Janeiro highlighted the role of women in implementing sustainable development practices and the importance of women's equality.
- The 1993 World Conference on Human Rights in Vienna affirmed that women's rights are human rights and, as such, must be assured.
- The 1994 International Conference on Population and Development in Cairo established specific goals for improving women's status and empowerment.
- The 1995 Social Summit in Copenhagen consolidated and reiterated themes of the previous conferences.
- The 1995 Fourth World Conference on Women in Beijing was the biggest and arguably the most significant global meeting to focus on reproductive rights.
- The 1996 Second Conference on Human Settlements in Istanbul made clear the connection between reproductive rights and creating sustainable human settlements.

Boland's report analyses the international community's recognition of reproductive rights, including women's role in reproductive decisions, and addresses guidelines required for positive future action.

The United Nations recognises the rights of families to determine the number and spacing of their children, as well as access to information and methods necessary to control fertility, and the right to make decisions about reproduction and sexuality. While these rights are receiving international attention, Boland cites a great need to determine and clarify their meaning in various cultures and regions.

Observing that accessibility and availability of reproductive health care justifies the attainment of full reproductive rights, the report stresses that techniques and services must be available to families, particularly women and children.

Boland further contends that governments that make family planning available and easily accessible reduce the incidence of unwanted pregnancy and abortion.

> *The elimination of violence against women is crucial to establishing their reproductive and basic human rights*

Governments can work to ensure safe motherhood by providing affordable maternal health services such as nutrition programmes, delivery services and prenatal and postnatal care.

The report cites the reproductive health needs of adolescents as another essential, yet often ignored, factor in reproductive health care. HIV/AIDS and sexually transmitted diseases, combined with a lack of knowledge of and control over their prevention and transmission, also threaten the reproductive health of men, women and children around the world.

The elimination of violence against women is crucial to establishing their reproductive and basic human rights, the report emphasises, noting that rape, prostitution, physical assault and mental cruelty occur in both developed and developing countries.

Boland points out that some cultures actually encourage violations of the rights of women and girls, such as genital mutilation and son preference. An international lack of respect for, or, in some cases, acknowledgement of, women's rights makes women vulnerable to acts of violence. Future progress on reproductive rights depends on the co-operation and action of the international community, governments and non-governmental organisations (NGOs) to promote these rights.

Boland's report provides the much needed direction for international, regional and national efforts to transform recently solidified international dedication to reproductive rights into effective strategies and programmes as we progress toward the twenty-first century.

IPPF Charter on Sexual and Reproductive Rights

In 1995, the International Planned Parenthood Federation and its 127 member associations approved a Charter on Sexual and Reproductive Rights, based on international human rights instruments. A summary follows:

1. The right to life should be invoked to protect women whose lives are currently endangered by pregnancy.

2. The right to liberty and security of the person should be invoked to protect women currently at risk from genital mutilation, or subject to forced pregnancy, sterilisation or abortion.

3. The right to equality and to be free from all forms of discrimination should be invoked to protect the right of all people, regardless of race, colour, sex, sexual orientation, marital status, family position, age, language, religion, political or other opinion, national or social origin, property, birth or other status, to equal access to information, education and services related to development, and to sexual and reproductive health.

4. The right to privacy should be invoked to protect the right of all clients to sexual and reproductive health care information, education and services to a degree of privacy, and to confidentiality with regard to personal information given to service providers.

5. The right to freedom of thought should be invoked to protect the right of all persons to access to education and information related to their sexual and reproductive health free from restrictions on grounds of thought, conscience and religion.

6. The right to information and education should be invoked to protect the right of all persons to access to full information on the benefits, risks and effectiveness of all methods of fertility regulation, in order that any decisions they take on such matters are made with full, free and informed consent.

7. The right to choose whether or not to marry and to found and plan a family should be invoked to protect all persons against any marriage entered into without the full, free and informed consent of both partners.

8. The right to decide whether or when to have children should be invoked to protect the right of all persons to reproductive health care services which offer the widest possible range of safe, effective and acceptable methods of fertility regulation, and are accessible, affordable, acceptable and convenient to all users.

9. The right to health care and health protection should be invoked to protect the right of all persons to the highest possible quality of health care, and the right to be free from traditional practices which are harmful to health.

10. The right to the benefits of scientific progress should be invoked to protect the right of all persons to access to available reproductive health care technology which independent studies have shown to have an acceptable risk/benefit profile, and where to withhold such technology would have harmful effects on health and well-being

11. The right to freedom of assembly and political participation should be invoked to protect the right to form an association which aims to promote sexual and reproductive health and rights.

12. The right to be free from torture and ill treatment should be invoked to protect children, women and men from all forms of sexual violence, exploitation and abuse.

© UNFPA

Reproductive rights

Information from the United Nations

Reproductive health and reproductive rights are relatively new concepts in the area of population policy. They are also a particularly controversial topic. They relate to areas of life that are the most intimate and personal, such as sexuality, sexual relations and reproduction, as well as to matters that are central to how the members of a family relate to one another and how they perceive themselves. They are also linked with the status of women and the empowerment of women, matters which themselves provoke controversy in many countries.

Reproductive rights may be viewed as certain rights that all persons possess which will allow them access to the full range of reproductive health care. In particular, as formulated at the past three international conferences on population and at the Fourth World Conference on Women, these rights rest on the recognition of the basic right of all couples and individuals to decide freely and responsibly the number, spacing and timing of their children and to have the information and means to do so. They include the right to attain the highest standard of sexual and reproductive health and the right to make reproductive decisions free from discrimination, coercion and violence, as expressed in human rights documents. Furthermore, the Programme of Action of the International Conference on Population and Development and the Platform for Action of the Fourth World Conference on Women, drawing upon the language originally formulated at the International Conference on Human Rights, held at Tehran in 1968, strongly support reproductive rights. Although the documents are not legally binding in terms of international law, they do bear great normative authority and have been endorsed by the vast majority of governments.

Formal international treaties that are legally binding also support the concept of reproductive rights, if not by name. For example, the International Covenant on Civil and Political Rights contains a number of provisions that are relevant to the right to make voluntary decisions about bearing children. Similarly, the International Covenant on Economics, Social and Cultural Rights recognises the right of persons to enjoy the highest standards of health and calls for special attention to be

---

Reproductive rights may be viewed as certain rights that all persons possess which will allow them access to the full range of reproductive health care

---

given to women before and after childbirth and to the reduction of infant mortality. With the approval of the Convention on the Elimination of All Forms of Discrimination against Women in 1979, those reproductive rights are made explicit and strongly endorsed. National laws that support reproductive rights relating to maternal/child health care, access to the various forms of family planning, sex education and treatment and prevention of sexually transmitted diseases are common in both developing and developed countries.

One of the cornerstones of the concept of reproductive rights is the right of access to methods of family planning. This idea has been fundamental to definitions of reproductive rights from the beginning, appearing repeatedly in population and human rights documents as the right to have the 'information and means' to decide freely and responsibly the number and spacing of children. Without such access, reproductive rights have, practically speaking, no real meaning.

Adolescent reproductive behaviour has become an emerging worldwide concern. Most countries do not have coherent policies for the protection and maintenance of reproductive health in adolescents, partly because of the sensitivity of the subject. Several key issues concerning the reproductive rights of adolescents pertain to marriage. In many parts of the world, women's basic human rights are violated when they are given in marriage without their consent. Moreover, despite legislation designed to eliminate the practice, girls in many countries marry shortly after puberty and are expected to start having children almost immediately, in part because of a lack of alternative opportunities. The adverse effects of early childbearing are not only biomedical but also educational and economic, in the form of reduced opportunities for young mothers.

Many obstacles exist to the achievement of reproductive rights and reproductive health. Because of the sensitive and controversial character of the issues involved – in particular, sexuality, contraception, the empowerment of women and family relations – there is resistance to the expansion of reproductive rights. Another major problem is conceptual in nature. In many countries, human and reproductive rights, as expressed in international documents, are not familiar to the general public and little information is disseminated on them. In addition, human and reproductive rights may seem abstract in their formulation or even foreign to local experiences, attitudes and traditions. The less educated are especially likely to lack knowledge about their rights. Also, women more than men are subject to restrictions on their personal status which prevent them from obtaining information on their rights. Thus, many women are not aware that they have reproductive rights and are therefore unlikely to exercise them.

Action to achieve reproductive rights and health is restricted in scope by those obstacles. However, one strategy to overcome such obstacles is to try to strengthen and make greater use of international monitoring mechanisms. Another is

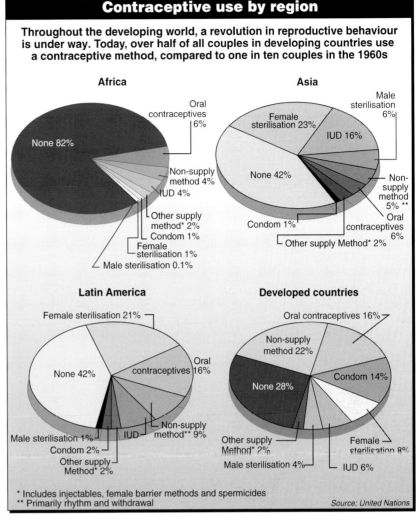

Contraceptive use by region

Throughout the developing world, a revolution in reproductive behaviour is under way. Today, over half of all couples in developing countries use a contraceptive method, compared to one in ten couples in the 1960s

Africa

None 82%

Oral contraceptives 6%

Non-supply method 4%

IUD 4%

Other supply method* 2%

Condom 1%

Female sterilisation 1%

Male sterilisation 0.1%

Asia

Male sterilisation 6%

Female sterilisation 23%

IUD 16%

None 42%

Non-supply method 5% **

Oral contraceptives 6%

Condom 1%

Other supply Method* 2%

Latin America

Female sterilisation 21%

None 42%

Oral contraceptives 16%

Non-supply method** 9%

Male sterilisation 1%

IUD

Condom 2%

Other supply Method* 2%

Developed countries

Oral contraceptives 16%

Non-supply method 22%

Condom 14%

None 28%

Other supply Method* 2%

Female sterilisation 8%

Male sterilisation 4%

IUD 6%

* Includes injectables, female barrier methods and spermicides
** Primarily rhythm and withdrawal

Source: United Nations

to increase the provision of information and education on reproductive rights and reproductive health. Efforts can be increased to reach the millions of persons throughout the world who have little knowledge or understanding of reproductive health. These efforts cover basic facts on health and the reproductive system and the connection between reproductive health and such matters as age at marriage, level of education, the status of women and harmful practices, such as female genital mutilation. Greater publicity can also be given to the existence at the international level of the documents that countries have ratified which support rights on such matters, particularly the right to decide freely and responsibly the number and spacing of children. Moreover, to be effective, this information should be provided to medical personnel, religious leaders, government officials and non-governmental organisations.

The concept of reproductive rights must be presented in ways that are appropriate to the local level. One approach is to point to local laws that themselves support reproductive rights, such as the constitutions, population policies and health laws of various countries. Another is to draw on local social movements and traditions that support reproductive rights. A third approach is to relate 'rights' language to actual needs at the local level – needs for basic health services, family planning and education, for example. If reproductive rights and reproductive health are to be secured at the local level, they need to be integrated into existing societal structures and thus become part of the fabric of society.

• The above is an extract from *Reproductive Rights and Reproductive Health: A concise report*, produced by the United Nations. See page 41 for address details.

© United Nations
New York, 1996

Family planning progress

Since family planning programmes were first launched in the 1960s, the percentage of women in developing countries (including China) using contraception has increased about fivefold and the average number of children born to each woman has fallen from six to three. But these figures mask a great deal of variation among regions and countries.

Monitoring Family Planning Programs 1996 is a compilation of much of the available data on the state of family planning programmes in 96 developing countries. This wallchart is the first to present a comparative country-by-country overview of family planning evaluation indicators.

Produced by the Carolina Population Center at Chapel Hill in collaboration with the Population Reference Bureau, the data range from government spending on family planning to the types of services available, the facilities used to deliver those services, and the number of new contraceptive users served each year. Key findings include the following:

Around the world, most governments are concerned about high birth rates.

Nearly 80 per cent of governments in Africa and over half of all governments in Latin America report that birth rates are too high. A notable exception is the high-fertility region of West Asia (including Iraq, Jordan, Yemen, and Syria) where most governments consider birth rates to be satisfactory, and family planning services have not been promoted as a means of reducing fertility. In East Asia, where family planning programmes have been in place for decades, fertility has fallen below replacement level (about two children per woman).

Family planning effort still lags in many countries. Of the 95 countries with family planning effort scores, only 41 received 'moderate' or 'strong' scores (50 to 92 per cent of the maximum score possible). Of all Latin American countries, 62 per cent ranked as either moderate or strong, compared with only 23 per cent of African countries. In Asia, just over half of all countries scored moderate or strong in family planning.

National and international spending on family planning is often insufficient. An alternative measure of a country's commitment to family planning is a government's annual per capita expenditure on family planning services. Based on available cost data, the very highest level of government spending is reported by Mauritius, where an average of US$1.65 per person is spent on family planning services or supplies. Several governments spent less than

US$0.01 per person, including Afghanistan, Brazil, the Congo, Honduras, Iran, Paraguay, Uganda, and Zaire. Total per capita spending on family planning (from all sources) is US$1 or more only in Costa Rica, El Salvador, Mauritius, Tunisia, and Zimbabwe.

Almost half of the married women in developing countries use a modern form of contraception. Regional data show a variety of different patterns, however. In Africa, only 17 per cent of married, reproductive-age women use a modern form of contraceptive, ranging from 11 per cent in Sub-Saharan Africa to 36 per cent in North Africa. Contraceptive prevalence is significantly higher in Asia and Latin America, ranging from a low of 34 per cent in South central Asia to 53 per cent in Latin America and a high of 78 per cent in East Asia.

Family planning service providers may be too few in number. The ratio of married women ages 15-44 per family planning staff member ranges from a high of 111,235 in the Ivory Coast to a low of 109 in Vietnam. Although the highest ratios of women per provider are found in Africa, several Latin American and Asian countries also have high ratios: of the 38 countries that have more than 1,000 women per staff member, 16 are in Africa, 12 in Latin America, and 10 in Asia.

• For a free single copy of the wallchart, contact the EVALUATION Project, Carolina Population Center, University of North Carolina, 123 West Franklin Street, Suite 304, CB #8120, University Square, Chapel Hill, NC 27516-3997. Phone (919) 966-7482; fax (919) 966-2391.

© *Population Today*
June, 1997

Percentage of Married Women Using Modern Contraceptives, Selected Countries

Mexico	56
Haiti	14
Jamaica	63
China	81
South Korea	70
Thailand	64
Vietnam	37
India	36
Egypt	46
Nigeria	4
Kenya	27

Note: Data refer to some point from 1987 to 1995.

Source: *Monitoring Family Planning Programs 1996*, drawn from Macro International's Demographic and Health Surveys and the United Nations Population Division, Contraceptive Use 1994.

UNFPA *stresses gender equality, maternal health*

The international community has agreed repeatedly that reproductive health is a right for both women and men, says Dr Nafis Sadik, Executive Director of the United Nations Population Fund (UNFPA). 'The challenge now is to make this right a reality for every individual.'

To enable individuals to exercise their sexual and reproductive rights, the Fund's State of World Population 1997 report stresses the need for gender equality and increased investment in education and primary health care.

Specific recommendations focus on improving the availability and quality of information and services that meet a broad range of sexual and reproductive health needs.

The report documents the effects of denying sexual and reproductive rights, including:

- 585,000 women – one every minute – die each year from pregnancy-related causes, nearly all in developing countries. Many times this number are disabled as the result of childbirth. Much of this death and suffering could be averted with relatively low-cost improvements in health care systems.
- About 200,000 maternal deaths per year result from the lack or failure of contraceptive services.
- 120-150 million women who want to limit or space their pregnancies are still without the means to do so effectively. Altogether 350 million couples lack information about and access to a range of contraceptive services.
- At least 75 million pregnancies each year (out of about 175 million) are unwanted; they result in 45 million abortions, 20 million of which are unsafe.
- 70,000 women die each year as a result of unsafe abortion, and an unknown number suffer infection and other health consequences. Many unsafe abortions could be avoided if safe and effective means of contraception were freely available.
- 120 million women have undergone some form of female genital mutilation; another 2 million are at risk each year.
- Rape and other forms of sexual violence are rampant, though many rapes are unreported because of the stigma and trauma associated with rape and the lack of sympathetic treatment from legal systems.
- At least 60 million girls who would otherwise be expected to be alive are 'missing' from various populations as a result of sex-selective abortions or neglect.
- 2 million girls between ages 5 and 11 are introduced into the commercial sex market each year.

The 1994 International Conference on Population and Development estimated that providing better reproductive health care world-wide will cost $17 billion annually by the year 2000 – less than the world currently spends each week on armaments.

But while many governments have increased their allocations for population programmes since 1994, annual global expenditures are still well below half the $17 billion mark.

The UNFPA report stresses that sexual and reproductive rights are key to women's empowerment and gender equality, and are also critical to the economic and social life of communities, nations and the world.

The report calls for greater attention to human rights, especially the promotion of gender equality and women's empowerment.

Achievement of these rights requires legal reforms, better enforcement of existing laws, new procedure to document violations, education about human rights, and alliances among institutions concerned with rights.

To combat the poverty that prevents the exercise of sexual and reproductive rights, the report advocates increasing women's access to credit and economic resources. It stresses the value of both general education and specific education on sexual and reproductive health.

The report calls for greater investment in primary health care, particularly for sexual and reproductive health. Health services should be restructured to focus on the reproductive and sexual health needs of clients, including underserved groups, using new guidelines, standards of conduct and evaluation methods.

United Nations, NY
© Popline
May/June, 1997

I'm the first man on the pill

All that worry about the right contraception may soon be over – we can leave it to the men. Brian McDonald, 32, a care worker from Edinburgh, is the first man to test the male Pill. Here he tells *Zest* how it feels to make medical history, as told to John Arlidge

It all started last October. I was about to have a vasectomy but I changed my mind at the last minute. I agreed to have the operation because, with two children – Mary, three, and Elizabeth, two – we thought our family was complete. Besides, Denise had had postnatal depression and I didn't want her to go through that again.

'I was lying on the operating table and the surgeon was halfway through when I suddenly thought, "I can't do this. I want to be able to have more children." I screamed at him to stop. He looked pretty surprised but he did stop. Then he assured me I would still be fertile. It was such a relief.

'But I still had a problem. Denise couldn't take the Pill, and other forms of contraception had proved tricky. Then I remembered the doctors at Edinburgh Royal Infirmary were looking for volunteers for the male Pill. I got in touch with them – it's the best thing I've ever done.

'I take one aspirin-sized pill, containing a synthetic version of the hormone progesterone, every day. It tricks my brain into stopping sperm production and it's said to be 99 per cent effective. The only side-effect is a decline in my testosterone levels. To reverse that, I get an injection every four to six months. If I stop taking the pill, I'll be fertile immediately.

'The Pill doesn't affect my behaviour, our lovemaking or my libido at all. The only off-putting aspect is the testosterone injections – I hope they'll soon be replaced by a tablet. Then, other men will have no excuse not to go on the Pill.

'It's great that men are being offered the chance to take control of their own fertility, and I'm very proud to be the first one to do it. Some men might see preventing sperm production as a threat to their masculinity but I certainly don't feel any less of a man. Women tell me I'm courageous but men seem nervous. Some even accused me of betraying my sex by "batting for the other side". I don't see it that way – if a woman can take the Pill, so can a man. I've been told I'm a sexual revolutionary: one newspaper even called me a feminist hero – if you knew me, you'd find that funny! In the end, people can say what they want. I am doing what I am doing for Denise and, as long as I don't get asked to appear on that awful *Girlie Show* programme, I don't mind.'

'And I'm the luckiest woman in Britain'

Brian's wife Denise, 27, is delighted with the arrangement. 'When it comes to family planning,' she says, 'men have had it too easy for too long. It's a relief that men like Brian can now play their full part. People tell me I'm the luckiest woman in Britain, not having to worry about contraception and it's true.

'The more contraceptive choices couples have, the better. I've suffered side-effects from taking the female Pill and the recent health scare over some brands really worried some of my friends. But taking the male Pill doesn't seem to effect men – Brian is still his same old self. But I do think the male Pill works best for those in a stable relationship because so much trust is involved. If I'd just met someone and, in the throes of passion, he whispered, "Trust me, darling, I'm on the Pill," I wouldn't necessarily believe him.

'Brian knows, if he forgot to take the Pill and I got pregnant, we'd both have to take responsibility for the child. That makes us extra careful. Every day, I ask him if he's taken his pill – it always makes us laugh.'

The male Pill
[your questions answered]

Dr Cameron Martin is Research Fellow and Head of Clinical Research at Edinburgh University's Centre of Reproductive Biology. We asked him to tell us more about his research into the male Pill…

How does it work?

'The Pill is a synthetic version of the hormone progesterone. It works by switching off a signal from the brain to the testes, reducing both sperm and testosterone production.'

How often does a man need to take it?

A man takes one pill a day. He also has a testosterone injection once every several months, to counteract any loss of the hormone when taking the Pill.'

Are there any side-effects?

'We haven't seen any to date, although there have only been short-term studies. However, there is a possibility of mood changes. We are currently starting a six to 12-month trial to try to establish definitely that there are no risks. We're confident the male Pill will prove to be safe for long-term use.'

© Zest
June, 1997

> 'It's great that men are being offered the chance to take control of their own fertility, and I'm very proud to be the first one to do it . . .'

Why Sandro has to keep taking the tablets

Enthusiastic revolutionary feels better than normal

Have you taken your pill, darling?' Carol Mallin asks her partner Sandro Centola.

It is a question thousands more women will be asking their husbands if Mr Centola proves the male pill is easy to use and effective.

Mr Centola, aged 38, a British Telecom engineer from Edinburgh, is one of hundreds of men taking part in a new contraceptive research project. In early tests he suffered no side-effects and he has thrown away his condoms to start taking the saccharine-sized tablet which he says has improved his sex life.

'When I take the pill I feel even better than normal. It makes me more relaxed, which makes our love-making better. I am sick of condoms. You can never find them when you need them and while you've got them on you worry that they might break. The pill is much better.'

Mr Centola volunteered to try out the drug after Carol had the couple's second child, Lara.

'We did not want more children and Carol did not want to go back on the pill because of the health risks. I thought about having a vasectomy but it was just too final, so when my doctor told me about the research project I said yes.'

Despite the recent health scare over popular brands of the female pill, Mr Centola says he has no doubts about the male version. 'I asked the doctors lots of questions and I trust their answers.

'I had no problems in the tests and can't see any difficulties.

'Men's bodies are simpler than women's so there is less risk of anything going wrong.'

Although relatives have teased him, calling him Sandra Jaffa, he is an enthusiastic sexual revolutionary.

'Women have always taken responsibility for birth control and I think it's time men did too. It will even up the balance. Stopping sperm production does not make me feel any less masculine.'

The testosterone implants are the only off-putting aspect of the new drug.

'My mood changes and Carol complains they turn me into a bit of a sex monster, but you don't have them any more often than you go to the dentist so we can cope with it.'

He is convinced that most men will be willing to take the pill. 'I am just an ordinary bloke and if I can do it, I'm sure others will too.'

Friends tell Carol, 39, that she is the luckiest woman in Britain, not having to worry about birth control, but she is still nervous.

'You hear the doctors say the pill reduces the sperm count to just 3 million per millilitre which they say is infertile, but you can't help thinking: "Well, it only takes one". As a nurse, though, I trust the doctors' judgement.'

But does she trust Sandro to take the pill? 'He's normally pretty good at remembering things but I'll be the one in trouble if he forgets. I'll be keeping an eye on the bottle.'

© The Guardian
October, 1997

How reliable are contraceptives?	
Male condom	95.0%
Female condom	95.0%
Female pill	99.0%
Coil or IUD	99.0%
Diaphragm	93.0%
Rhythm method	87.0%
Vasectomy	99.9%
Female sterilisation	99.7%
Hormone implants	99.0%
Male pill	99.0%

Pill for men blasted by Catholic groups

By Lynne Thorabie

Critics have condemned the prospect of the first 'safe' male contraceptive pill, which could be dominating the market within five years.

The Society for the Protection of Unborn Children told the *Herald*: 'Something which persistently suppresses a natural function could be very dangerous; in the same way they found that persistent suppression with the Pill has had serious effect on women's health.'

Family and Youth Concern said: 'We know that the female contraceptive pill is not safe; even after 30 years of this pill, how safe is this male pill? Personally, I am sceptical about the fact most men can scarcely bring themselves to have aspirins.'

The pill, which was tested on 30 young men over four months, made them temporarily infertile, but gave no significant side-effects. Within days of the treatment ending, they were producing healthy sperm. Dr Cameron Martin, who has led the programme at the Medical Research Council reproductive biology unit in Edinburgh, announced the full results on Wednesday to 2,500 delegates at a meeting of the European Society of Human Reproduction and Embryology in the city.

For doctors, the daily pill contains progesterone, a naturally occurring human hormone. An injection every three months releases testosterone into the system to compensate for the body's temporary failure to produce it. The injected testosterone cannot cross back into the testes. So it fails to stimulate sperm production.

Previous treatments, although effective in preventing pregnancy, have been found to cause serious side-effects.

*© Catholic Herald
June, 1997*

The truth about vasectomy

'The snip' has been a convenient and popular form of contraception since the sixties. But is the operation always effective? And are there any risks?
By Cherrill Hicks

Child-hating *ER* hunk' George Clooney is keen on it, according to the tabloids. Bishop Philip Boyce of Rathoe, Donegal, has branded it as 'against God's law.' One man, writing to *The Sun's* 'Dear Deirdre' column, said it had sent his sex drive 'through the roof'; another complained it had made his wife too randy. A woman at an auction in Devon, meanwhile, bought it for £70 as a present for her husband.

Vasectomy, or male sterilisation, introduced in Britain in the sixties, is fast becoming a popular contraceptive option, with about 90,000 men undergoing the operation annually (although according to one London clinic, it is usually the women who suggests it). In the last few years, some men have been put off 'the snip' by studies suggesting a link with cardiovascular disease and cancer. But a report on vasectomy published this month is, for the most part, reassuring.

The operation itself, widely available on the NHS, is simple and safe enough; carried out under local anaesthetic, it involves cutting the vas deferens, the tube that carries

Vasectomy, or male sterilisation, introduced in Britain in the Sixties, is fast becoming a popular contraceptive option

sperm from each testicle to the penis. A small cut is made in the skin of the scrotum and either a small piece of each tube is removed, or the tubes are cut and the ends closed. The operation takes about 10 minutes and usually results in some bruising and tenderness (tight underpants help). Slight bleeding may occur; in some cases, sperm leaks out of the tube and collects in surrounding tissue, causing inflammation. Most men, however, return to work within a few days and resume sex within a week to 10 days, although they need to use another method of contraception until sperm left in the tubes have been ejaculated. Only after semen has been analysed and found to be sperm-free is a man considered sterile.

Despite male fears that it makes a man less 'manly', vasectomy does not normally affect the ability to ejaculate or come to orgasm; although it blocks the passage of sperm, it has no effect on the glands secreting fluids that form most of the semen. Since the testicles still produce male sex hormone, a man's sex drive and ability to have an erection should not be affected.

Vasectomy is a highly effective method of contraception, though in up to five cases in every 1,000 the severed parts of the tube reunite and sperm reappear, necessitating further surgery. But in the long term, is it safe?

Most of the scares associated with vasectomy have been shown to be without foundation. In the eighties, animal studies linked vasectomy to cardiovascular problems, but to date there is no evidence of this in research using humans. A suggested link between vasectomy and testicular cancer has not been substantiated. Several studies have indicated that prostate cancer may be twice as common among vasectomised men, but other studies do not show this; most experts feel that the risk, if any, is small. In the 65-74 age group about 3 men per 1,000 in Britain develop the disease. If the risk were doubled for vasectomised men, this would mean 6 vasectomised men per 1,000 per year. In this age group, the chances of dying from another cause are five times greater.

The new review of research, published in the *British Journal of*

General Practice, points out that the effects of vasectomy on the reproductive tract, particularly the testicles, are not well understood: a small group of men develop chronic discomfort and testicular pain, probably caused by scar tissue forming around the nerves. The psychological effects of vasectomy are less well documented. In a detailed study of 68 men who had had vasectomies, about 10 years previously, published in the *British Journal of Family Planning*, 12 per cent said it had impaired their orgasmic intensity, erectile function and sex drive (while that of their wives had increased); only 61 per cent felt that sexual function was completely undisturbed. The majority of such problems are thought to be psychological (and could well be the result of ageing rather than surgery), which is why it is crucial that anyone considering vasectomy should undergo counselling.

About 3 per cent of vasectomy patients later change their minds about having a family, usually because they have changed their partners. Reversing the operation, although complicated (and costly – it is available only privately, for about £1,000), is more successful than in the past, thanks to new techniques using microsurgery. If a reversal is carried out within three years of the original operation, success rates – (i.e., the woman getting pregnant) – can be as high as 76 per cent; after 15 years they fall to less than 30 per cent. Many men produce antibodies to their own sperm once they have had a vasectomy, and therefore suffer from low fertility following reversal, although some doctors are now using IVF to overcome this problem.

*© The Independent
June, 1997*

The human right

Family planning and sexual and reproductive health

Notable dates in the development of rights to family planning and sexual and reproductive health
1968 UN International Conference on Human rights (Tehran)
The Tehran Declaration stated that parents had the basic human right to decide freely and responsibly on the number and spacing of their children

and a right to adequate education and information

1974 World Population Conference (Bucharest)
This conference gave the right to family planning to couples and individuals, rather than parents, and stated the right to the means – as

well as to information and education – to decide the number and spacing of children.

1978 International Conference on Primary Health Care (USSR)
The Alma Ata Declaration established family planning as part of maternal and child health care.

1979 UN Convention on the Elimination of All Forms of Discrimination Against Women
The convention emphasised equality between men and women in their right and ability to control reproduction. It required member states to eliminate discrimination against women in the exercise of their right to health care, including family planning, and in all matters relating to marriage and family relations.

1984 UN International Conference on Population (Mexico City)
Recommendations from the Mexico population conference stated that it was a matter of urgency for governments to make universally available information, education and the means to assist couples and individuals to achieve their desired number of children. Family planning should include all medically approved methods and particular attention should be given to those hard to reach. For the first time, governments were asked to meet the needs of adolescents for adequate family life and sex education and to make available appropriate services.

1985 Forward-Looking Strategies for the Advancement of Women (Nairobi)
Adolescent girls were identified as a significant group at risk of unwanted pregnancy and in special need of government attention.

1993 UN World Conference on Human Rights (Vienna)
The Vienna Declaration for the first time specified that the human rights of women and of the girl child were an inalienable, integral and indivisible part of universal human rights. The declaration reaffirmed a woman's right to accessible and adequate health care and the widest range of family planning services. Also for the first time, violence against women was recognised as a human rights abuse.

1994 International Conference on Population and Development (ICPD) (Cairo)
The ICPD Programme of Action established the right of couples and individuals to attain the highest standard of reproductive health, which was defined as including sexual health and family planning. The conference reiterated the right to make decisions concerning reproduction free of discrimination, coercion and violence, as expressed in human rights documents, and stated that the promotion of the responsible exercise of these rights for all people should be the fundamental basis for government and community-supported policies and programmes in the area of reproductive health. The conference made it a goal to achieve universal access to a full range of safe and reliable family planning methods, and to related reproductive health services, by 2015. Programmes for adolescents should include education and counselling on gender relations and equality, responsible family planning practice, reproductive health and sexually transmitted diseases and HIV/AIDS prevention. Govern-

ments were urged to deal with unsafe abortion as a major public health concern.

1995 Fourth World Conference on Women (Beijing)
The Platform for Action urged governments to ensure the full implementation of the human rights of women and of the girl child. The right of all women to control all aspects of their health, in particular their fertility, was said to be basic to their empowerment. The document stated that reproductive health and family planning programmes should include education and awareness-raising about reproductive rights as human rights.

The conference recognised a distinction between women's rights in relation to their sexuality and those related to reproduction. Female genital mutilation was classified as violence against women and therefore a violation of their human rights. Governments were urged to review laws containing punitive measures against women who had undergone illegal abortion.
• The above is an extract from *The human right to family planning and sexual and reproductive health*, produced by the International Planned Parenthood Federation. See page 41 for address details.

© IPPF

Mothers in waiting

'Thirty somethings' go back on the pill to keep family options open

By Jenny Hope,
Medical Correspondent

Women in their 30s and 40s are going back on the pill to stay in control of their lives, a survey says.

It found the pill remains women's favourite method of family planning – used by 3.8 million – but new trends are emerging at different ages.

More women in their 30s and 40s are using the pill than ever before. The proportion aged 30-34 is 29 per cent, up two per cent since 1993, and with those aged 35-44 it is up five points at 16 per cent. From the statistics, it appears women are having children in their mid to late 20s. But when they reach their 30s they are going back on the pill to keep their options open.

Gynaecologist David Paintin, of the Birth Control Trust, said trends in pill use now showed a 'ripple effect'. 'These older women are achieving in life and they appreciate the close control over fertility given by the pill and its reversibility. They may want to have more children.'

But the pill also has side benefits such as reducing period problems and pre-menstrual depression, he said.

'These things are important to women in their 30s and 40s who are holding down a job and earning a fair amount of money. They well offset the slight increase in medical risks of the pill in this age group.' Anne Weyman, of the Family Planning Association, said: 'Women in their 20s are beginning to have families but afterwards they are not choosing methods of family planning that are non-reversible, like sterilisation.'

The NOP survey found that the scare last October over a slightly higher risk of blood clots linked to a new generation of pill has barely dented its popularity – except among women in their 20s. Pill use among

> *More women in their 30s and 40s are using the pill than ever before. The proportion aged 30-34 is 29 per cent, up two per cent since 1993*

women aged 25-29 is down by a quarter, with a less sharp decline among women in their early 20s.

Teenage girls are also major users of the pill, up from 40 per cent to 43 per cent, partly because of their mothers' influence.

The sixties generation of women who first had access to the pill are now providing role models for their daughters and bridging the divide over sex which separated older generations.

The survey, for pill manufacturers Schering Health Care, also discovered that almost a million sexually active women in Britain do not use any contraception.

© The Daily Mail
September, 1996

Access to contraception

Percentage of the population with easy access to contraceptive methods

Region	Steriliation Female	Male	IUD	Pill	Condom	No. of countries
Less developed regions	61	47	61	64	66	93
Africa	17	9	33	54	51	35
Northern Africa	11	5	47	80	45	
Other Africa	18	10	28	46	53	
Asia	69	57	68	64	69	33
Eastern Asia	88	71	89	72	71	
South-central Asia	34	34	59	61	61	
South-eastern Asia	66	55	51	55	71	
Western Asia	28	8	59	74	63	
Latin America and the Caribbean	64	35	52	78	65	24

Source: United Nations, World Population Monitoring, 1996

Men take responsibility for reproductive health and family planning

Women point their fingers at men and say. 'We are willing to use family planning but these people prevent us from doing so.' Emmanual Sabakati has heard this lament often while counselling couples on family planning. Sabakati is project director of the 'Man to Man' programme in Malawi, designed to address the critical role of men in family planning.

But studies show than men are concerned for women's reproductive health, and are willing to participate in making decisions, according to *The State of World Population 1997* report by the United Nations Population Fund (UNFPA). The problem may be communications: husband and wife may want the same thing, but they don't tell each other. The result can be a bigger family than either really wanted.

Husband and wife communications about reproductive health, including family planning, has been improving over the past few decades, the report notes. However, a large minority of men still consider sexual and reproductive health to be exclusively women's concerns – so they don't discuss it. Worse, men often impede women's efforts at family planning, as the women in Sabakati's clinic charge. Dr. Everald Hosein coordinates the University of the West Indies Caribbean Population and Family Health Programming in Port of Spain, Trinidad and Tobago. He says that almost every method of contraception a woman might choose can be opposed by her partner for one reason or another. For example, some men complain that condoms and intra-uterine devices interfere with their sexual pleasure. One woman told Hosein. 'My man doesn't want me to use the pill. He says it will make me fat.'

The report finds that men are frequently insensitive to women's reproductive and sexual health needs. In many cultures misunderstandings and myths about female sexuality and reproductive systems persist – though there are indications that male attitudes towards a range of taboos (including concerns about menstruation and 'cleanliness') are changing.

Boys and men should be taught about responsible sexuality and parenthood, the report recommends. They need to understand the risks women face from pregnancy and childbirth, and from multiple partners, harmful traditional practices, and sexual initiation too early in life. Women's reproductive and sexual health requires the mutual concern and investment of both partners.

Man to Man was founded in response to these needs. Says Sabakati, 'It is important to target males because they are the heads of families, and therefore they should know about family planning.' Participants are taught abut various methods of contraception, particularly those men can use. 'When men are motivated to seek methods suitable for them, they choose between vasectomy or condoms,' notes Sabakati. All choices are strictly voluntary. 'If they choose condoms, we supply them. If they choose vasectomy, we assist in arranging it.' Those who undergo vasectomy are usually in their late thirties or early forties.

When he was a Boy Scout in Zimbabwe, Joseph Mabuto received family life education. The experience 'gave a new dimension to my life,' he said. Now a scout leader, Mabuto advises teenage scouts about family and reproductive matters. '[My scouts are always coming to me to ask about sexuality, maturity, peer pressure and the like,' he says.

Zimbabwe's Chief Scout Commissioner, Ignatius Kajenga, points out that the whole society benefits from providing family life education to boys. 'The boys disseminate the information to their family and friends, We teach them about sexuality, sexual health, sexually transmitted diseases including AIDS, and family [planning,' Most courses are conducted in local languages.

'Decision-making is an important aspect of the education,' Kajenga says. 'Eventually it is incumbent upon the boys themselves to make up their mind on what types on families they are going to have.' He adds that the boys are glad to receive information on sexuality and reproduction, as such subjects are generally taboo with parents.

Legal barriers also underscore the important role men play in family planning, according to the report. Fourteen countries require a woman to get her husband's consent before she can receive any contraceptive service. This has the effect of denying services to unmarried women, including adolescents and the divorced or widowed, as well as women who wish to delay or limit births but who cannot persuade their husbands. An additional 60 countries require spousal authorization for permanent methods. Spousal consent restrictions often apply to only to women, the report notes.

But the report finds signs of improvement, especially at the grassroots. In the Philippines, a new centre for men is experimenting with innovative ways to involve men in reproductive health programmes. In Indonesia, the government plans to expand its counselling programme to include training materials on male participation in family planning and reproductive health. In Ghana, seminars and plays have been organised for both male and female audiences to generate discussion on partners' joint responsibility in the use of family planning, parenting and family life.

The Noor Al Hussein Foundation in Jordan has launched a two-year nationwide motivational campaign with 'Family health is a joint responsibility of both spouses' as its slogan. The campaign, begun in April 1996, includes a wide range of activities: puppet shows, seminars, a mobile science exhibition, counselling and interactive educational theatre. Special activities are intended to sensitize men about their responsibilities in family planning and reproductive health.

Efforts to reach men are eliciting a response. 'When I read in the paper about the vasectomy, I was very much interested because I wanted to give relief to my wife,' said Aaron Kumwenda, a client at the Man to Man project in Malawi. 'Having had four children, she was tired, I thought. As the head of the family, I had to do it.'

Anderson Mazengera, who underwent the same procedure after deciding with his wife that they had reached their desired family size, noted that male responsibility does not end with vasectomy: 'Now what we have to do is develop our family.'

Childless women set to double

By Celia Hall, Medical Editor

The number of fertile women without children will nearly double from the current 13 per cent within the next 15 years, according to Government statisticians.

They predict that the population of Britain is set to fall for the first time since the Black Death.

Apart from a dip in the population in 1983, the trend has been upwards since records began and has grown steady in recent years.

The birth statistics suggest that the number of women born between 1964 and 1969 who will not have had children by the end of their reproductive life will rise to 20 per cent of the female population now aged 25-29, by 2010.

Bob Armitage, head of the fertility unit at the Office of National Statistics, said that live births, or the fertility rate, were the main factor in determining population size and the fertility rate in Britain had been in steady decline for 20 years.

'Childlessness is on the increase. It is a problem. We are likely to have a population which is more heavily weighted towards the elderly and with fewer workers in it,' he said.

Women might opt for childlessness because of an increase in job opportunities, he added.

While women today have on average 1.8 children, a rate of 2.1 is needed to sustain the population.

The population itself has not fallen so far, because people are living longer and because the number of women born in the mid to late 1960s – daughters of the post-war baby-boom mothers – is disproportionately large.

The data published yesterday in the latest edition of *Population Trends* shows that a third of births are to unmarried women but the fathers are not absent. This rise in babies born outside marriage has increased from seven per cent in 1964 to 32 per cent in 1994.

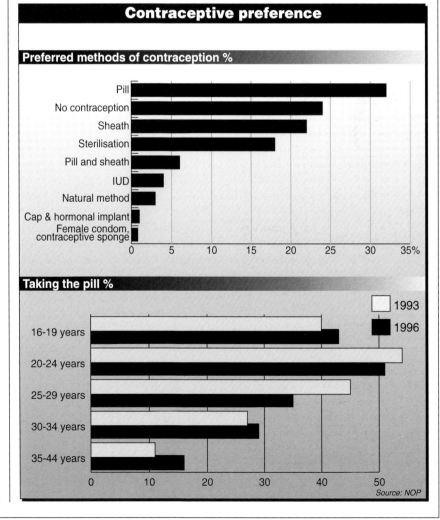

Contraceptive preference

Preferred methods of contraception %

Taking the pill %

Source: NOP

Fact or fiction?

Information from Actionaid

'People in Third World countries are poor because they have too many children'

There is no simple correlation between poverty and population. Some very wealthy countries have much higher fertility rates than the poorest countries. In Asia, for example, Oman (7.2), Saudi Arabia (6.4) and Syria (5.1) all have fertility rates that are much higher than Bangladesh (4.4) and India (3.8). In general, it is undoubtedly the case that countries with very high levels of human and economic development have much lower fertility rates – the US (2.1), Japan (1.5), the UK (1.8). But poverty and wealth on their own do not explain reproduction rates in any given country: it is much more meaningful to look at the issue of choice of women.

Both extended family and marital traditions play an important social, economic and welfare role in many poor countries. They can have a major influence on a woman's reproductive choices. Parents rely on their children for their care and protection in old age, for example. And marriage conventions place an economic premium on children's gender.

Against this background, high infant and child mortality rates mean that a mother who stops having children after her second or third child is in a precarious position. Child mortality rates are such that, in some of the poorest countries, there is a 20 to 30 per cent chance of a child dying before the age of five. These are only averages – many families in the very poorest areas of these countries experience far worse rates and the death of older children.

When it is quite possible that as many as half of the children born in a family will not reach full adulthood, and with the future economic security of parents being reliant on children, fertility rates of six or seven children can be seen in context.

> *In countries where health and family planning services have become relatively available, fertility rates have been seen to drop*

Undoubtedly there are links between population and poverty at a macro-level, but, to the extent that there is a causal relationship, poverty is the cause rather than the other way around. Breaking the cycle of rapid population growth and poverty requires the creation of conditions where child survival is more certain, with families having greater assurance of their future well-being and security, and where women are able to exercise choice in family planning.

Informed contraceptive choice is a fact of life in industrialised countries and, increasingly, in the Asian 'tiger economies'. But such choice is not available to many women in the poorest countries. In rural areas of Sub-Saharan Africa, only 49 per cent of the population have access to health services. According to the United Nations Population Fund, 120 million women in the developing world would like to plan their families but family planning advice is simply not available.

In countries where health and family planning services have become relatively available, fertility rates have been seen to drop. In Zimbabwe, for example, fertility rates fell from 7.5 in 1960 to 5.3 in 1993. During the same time span fertility rates dropped from 6.7 to 4.7 in Bangladesh and from 5.3 to 2.5 in Sri Lanka (UNICEF, *The State of World's Children*, 1995). These figures clearly show that with access to good quality family planning advice, women opt for smaller families. They also reinforce the conclusion that it is woefully simplistic to blame the size of families in the Third World for poverty.

© *Actionaid*

Health and choice and rights on the UK Government agenda

On the eve of World Population Day this year, the Rt Hon Clare Short MP, UK Secretary of State for International Development, was a guest of honour at a joint Population Concern/All-Party Group of Population, Development and Reproductive Health reception where she outlined the UK Government's commitments and priorities in international support to family planning and reproductive health. A slightly edited version of her speech appears here.

'At the dawn of a new millennium it is right that we should take stock and be clear about the kind of world we want to create for our grandchildren to inherit, and the actions we need to take to bring this about. I want to try to dispel the gloom that too frequently shrouds thinking about development and the future – a gloom which despondently says it is all outside our control. This is often the feeling when population is discussed. But I believe we can enable choices to be made which make a real difference.

'Whilst the last 30 years has seen progress in the numbers of couples able to benefit from family planning, there are still at least some 120 million without access to contraception. More than 90% of all people with AIDS live in the developing world – a clear indication that HIV is a disease of the poor and marginalised. Women, and especially young women, are at particular risk of HIV and other sexually transmitted diseases.

'At the dawn of a new millennium it is right that we should take stock and be clear about the kind of world we want to create for our grandchildren to inherit'

'These are challenges we face to make people's lives better now. But there is a bigger imperative – the shape of the future. We must take responsibility for protecting the global environment. We must work for early stabilisation of world population. These goals are not beyond our collective control. We must strive for them. It is the only way to offer a decent future to the generations to come. This means we must contribute to rapid stabilisation of world population. It is within our collective ability to reach this at around 10 billion rather than 15 billion. This is essential if we are to safeguard the world for the children of today's children.

What does all this mean in practice?

'It means meeting unmet demands for sexual and reproductive health. It means enabling women and men, particularly those who are poor, to benefit from a choice of sexual and reproductive health care and services. It means women being able to make choices about sex, pregnancy and childbirth free from the risks of injury or infection. It means increasing people's opportunity to determine and have control over their own futures. We have to make it a basic human right for women and men to choose, and to make the exercising of that right a reality.

'It also means meeting the needs of young people. Young people have traditionally been overlooked by, and receive little benefit from, the

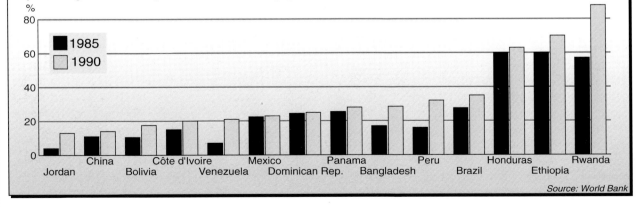

Percentage of population in absolute poverty in 1985 and 1990

An estimated 20 per cent to 25 per cent of the world's population live in 'absolute poverty', defined as per capita income of less than $370 a year. More than 90 per cent of such people live in developing countries, which are experiencing more than 90 per cent of the world's population growth.

Source: World Bank

reproductive health care and services that are available. Yet today's young people represent the largest generation in human history. The decisions and choices they make will largely determine whether world population stabilises at 10 billion people or 15 billion. We cannot any longer afford to treat young people's needs as peripheral or too delicate.

'Our efforts must be coherent and co-ordinated. Our role should be to support and complement partner countries based on an open and agreed agenda – but owned by our developing country partners. We must work closely with other donors and multilateral agencies on these partnerships with a clear understanding of needs, and agreement of the core principles that underpin our goals for human development.

'Our efforts must also be measurable. In the Development Assistance Committee (DAC) *Shaping the Twenty-first Century* report, we have measurable targets – many of which are familiar to those who have read the Cairo and Beijing programmes – against which collective progress can be measured. And it is important that our efforts should be monitored. The United Nations has a special role and will be an important partner for the UK. I also believe that the prospects for meeting the DAC and Cairo targets are likely to be improved by having a more strategic approach in alliance with donors and partner countries.

'We will build on past achievements. Our expenditure on population-related activities has more than doubled over the past few years, reaching £70 million in 1996.

'We can confront poverty to ensure that all women and men should have the basics for life – such as drinking water, shelter, fuel and food – and are able to benefit from the care and services that enable them to combat the threats to healthy living. One person in four lives on the equivalent of less than 65p a day. One and a half billion people lack access to safe water. Two billion lack safe sanitation. More than one billion people are illiterate. They lack the opportunities that might enable

them to have a better life. They are excluded from their real humanity.

'Women suffer the most. A key to poverty reduction must be to increase equality between women and men. Without achieving this, we are not likely to succeed in achieving sustainable improvements in people's lives. The contrasts between rich and poor are starkly highlighted by the differences in people's reproductive health. The poor, especially poor women, face huge obstacles to access services and care. They are disqualified from exercising choice about reproduction. They cannot bear their children in safety. They cannot protect themselves from infection. In Africa, one pregnancy in every 100 ends in the mother's death. In the UK, the figure is one in about 11,000. In many countries, a woman's lifetime risk of death related to pregnancy and childbirth for want of essential obstetric care is one in 20 or even as high as one in 12 in parts of Eastern Africa. The risk in the UK is one in 5,100. For every woman who dies in childbirth, 30 more suffer serious illness and often permanent disability.

What are our priorities?

'Priority number one is that we must increase the numbers of women and men, and young people, who are able to gain access to and benefit from the essential requirements for better sexual and reproductive health – information, services and commodities. People need the information which enables them to make choices and the capacity to exercise those choices. They also need contraceptives and other essential commodities. Here there is of course a special role for UNFPA which is taking a lead in the international effort.

Without better access to improved basic obstetric care for those who need it, women will continue to die in pregnancy and childbirth

---

'Condom promotion is still the only effective way we have of preventing HIV transmission and it is therefore essential that people should be easily able to get hold of condoms from a variety of sources. We must make sure that people are able to access the commodities and drugs they need to avoid, or have treated, sexually transmitted infections. Wherever possible, it means that women seeking contraception also have the care, attention and counselling needed to help protect their sexual health. We also need to develop methods additional to the condom for preventing the sexual transmission of infections. There is an urgent need for an effective virucide. We will contribute to this effort.

'Nowhere are the obstacles faced by women to health – and the inequalities faced by poor women – revealed more starkly than in the figure I cited earlier for maternal mortality. The tragedy and indecency is that we know the major causes of maternal mortality, and the kind of care that pregnant women need when things go wrong. Without better access to improved basic obstetric care for those who need it, women will continue to die in pregnancy and childbirth. We must do better. These are not principally matters of science. They are matters of political and moral choice and will.

'I am pleased to say that I have just approved an initiative in Malawi to support the Government's Safe Motherhood Programme. The Department for International Development (DFID) will provide just over £9 million over the next six years to implement the national programme in half the country. This will include improving access to better quality obstetric care.

Minimising the need for abortion

'In talking about maternal mortality, we also need to recognise the uncomfortable and visceral reality that many women die for want of safe abortion. Many others suffer the consequences of incomplete abortion – often performed in the most dreadful, unhygienic circumstances.

There are many reasons why women decide to have an abortion. For some, continuous childbearing becomes unbearable.

'Those who refuse access to effective contraception should not dare to make a fuss about abortion. Much of the demand for abortion is their fault. We should minimise the need for abortion. But we should also recognise that the women concerned should be able to make their own moral choices. Abortion should never be promoted as a means for family planning. This is one of the most unforgivable features of the former Soviet system. However, given that in practice many women will reach the decision to have their pregnancies terminated, we should work with partner countries to ensure that abortion services are safe, offered in a way that respects women's rights and dignity and within reach of women who need them.

'The international development agenda sets out clear goals for the world of the future. We must get the world to agree to these goals and to monitor progress in achieving them, at global, regional and national levels. Important targets are those for ensuring reproductive health care for all by 2015 and to reducing by three-quarters maternal mortality by the same date. They are ambitious targets, but so is the prize – a world fit to meet the hopes and aspirations of those who are now very small. If we do not act, we will reap the whirlwind. I am sure the agenda we have set ourselves can succeed, and if we fail our heritage to the world will be widespread catastrophe.'

© Choices
Vol. 26, 1997

Today's choices – tomorrow's population

Among the most important needs is universal access to the information and means to plan families

The rate of world population growth is already declining, but the number of people could still double or even triple from today's 5.8 billion before stabilising a century or more from now. Women in most countries are still having more than the two-child average consistent with a stable population size. Moreover, so many young people are now entering or moving through their childbearing years that even a two-child average per couple would still boost population size for a few decades until the momentum from past growth subsides. Yet there is reason for optimism. The combination of access to family planning and other reproductive health services, education for girls and economic opportunity for women could lower birth rates enough to stabilise world population well before a doubling of today's total.

At the 1994 International Conference on Population and Development in Cairo, 180 nations reached a historic consensus on both the need and the means to slow population growth and eventually stabilise human numbers. The strategy is grounded in the recognition that couples have the right to make their own decisions about childbearing. Among the most important needs is universal access to the information and means to plan families. The availability of a variety of contraceptive options helps women plan their families and avoid the health risks of unwanted pregnancies. Child spacing also makes it more likely that children will survive birth and the first few

years of life. In the long term, access to contraception helps reduce reliance on abortion, to which many women without access to effective contraception turn.

Both the ongoing decline in desired family size and the annual addition of 24 million more women in their childbearing years argue for dramatic expansion of international family planning and related health services in the coming years. Sharing expertise in contraception and family planning service delivery is consistent with the history, culture and ideals of industrialised nations. American, European and Japanese innovations in aviation, automobiles, televisions and computers are rapidly transforming the developing world, for good or ill. And these countries' expertise in public health, medicine and in providing clean water helped produce the unprecedented world-wide declines in death rates after World War II, the decisive factor in post-war population growth. Finally, industrialised countries increasingly are exporting their culture to poorer countries in the form of popular entertainment and advertising. These countries have an obligation to share as well as their technological advantages in contraception and reproductive health care. These are not affordable by most couples in developing countries without help from governments – their own and those of wealthier nations.

International family planning assistance represents a success story of historic proportions. In the 30 years since the United States and a few European governments began helping other countries provide their citizens with family planning services, the number of couples using contraception in developing countries has multiplied tenfold and the average number of children per woman has declined from nearly six to fewer than four. Population growth has slowed impressively, and it continues to grow.

All countries can also help slow population growth by improving the lives of women and girls in ways that go beyond providing access to family planning and related reproductive health care. Greater access to schooling for girls and young women – especially beyond the early grades – leads to lower birth rates in almost all countries and cultures. A secondary school education correlates with later marriage, knowledge and use of contraception and small family size. Secondary schooling also increases the likelihood that women will take paying jobs or launch small businesses and otherwise contributes more to their families, to their communities and to national economics. In addition, education for girls and women improves the survival rates of mothers and children, as parents' knowledge about preventative care is one of the most important contributors to family health.

In Peru, a woman who has completed 10 years of education typically has two or three children. A woman who has never seen a classroom has seven or eight. In 23

developing nations, the average women with a secondary school education has her first child three and a half years later in life than a woman with no schooling. Like smaller families, such delays in first births exert a powerful brake on population momentum by lengthening the time span between generations.[1] Average family size and child death rates are lowest in countries such as South Korea and Sri Lanka that combine high levels of education for women with strong family planning and health programmes.[2]

Greater access to schooling for girls and young women – especially beyond the early grades – leads to lower birth rates in almost all countries and cultures

---

Providing opportunities for women to gain income for their work enhances their status and well-being, and early evidence suggests that this, too, may encourage the use of family planning and thus contribute to slower population growth.[3] Banks in Asia and Latin America that provide small loans for women's enterprises find that women taking advantage of such programmes tend to have fewer children on average. (They also have much better repayment rates than men.) The World Bank, known more for the large development projects it helps sponsor than for its social sector spending, recently announced that it will lead a drive to raise $200 million to provide small-scale loans to help low income people start their own businesses, in part because the impacts of such loans on women's lives appears to be so positive.[4]

Family planning and related health services, education for girls and economic opportunity for women all work best when they work together, and each strategy deserves attention and financial resources. All governments need to expand access to family planning and other

reproductive health services, and to provide education for girls and economic opportunities for women world-wide.

A final word

Population matters – to those who want their children to live long and healthy lives, to those who value a clean and secure environment, to those who want to help others take responsibility for their own lives, to those who ask that jobs be available for all, and to those who work for a more peaceful world. Slowing world population growth is important to everyone. The 30-year effort to make contraception and related health and education services available world-wide is a success story. Today that success is threatened as never before by misunderstanding and misinformation. By informing yourself and communicating your views to legislators, national leaders and the news media, you can make a difference.

Sources:
1 T.P Schultz, *Return to Women's Education*, in E. King and A. Hill, *Women's Education in Developing Countries: Barriers, Benefits and Policies* (Baltimore, Maryland: Johns Hopkins University Press, 1991).
2 Shanti Conly, *Closing the Gender Gap: Educating Girls* (Washington, D.C.: Population Action International, 1993).
3 Sidney Ruth Schuler and Syed M. Hashemi, 'Credit Programs, Women's Empowerment, and Contraceptive Use in Rural Bangladesh,' *Studies in Family Planning*, Vol. 25, No. 2 (March-April 1994); Sidney R. Schuler, 'Empowerment and Family Planning in Bangladesh,' *Network*, Vol. 15, No. 1 (August 1994).
4 Christopher S. Wren, 'World Bank Plans Small Loans to Poor,' *The New York Times*, 17 July 1995.

• The above is an extract from *Why Population Matters*, produced by Population Action International. See page 41 for address details.

ADDITIONAL RESOURCES

You might like to contact the following organisations for further information. Due to the increasing cost of postage, many organisations cannot respond to enquiries unless they receive a stamped, addressed envelope.

Actionaid
Hamlyn House
MacDonald Road
London, N19 5PG
Tel: 0171 281 4101
Fax: 0171 281 5146
A charity working with children, families and communities to improve the quality of life in some of the poorest parts of the world. Produces publications including reports, case studies and activity packs, multimedia, video packs, maps and reference books. Ask for the publications list.

Alan Guttmacher Institute
120 Wall Street
New York NY 10005
USA
Tel: 001 212 248 1111
Fax: 001 212 248 1952
A non-profit organisation for reproductive health research which produces useful reports.

Birth Control Trust (BCT)
27-35 Mortimer Street
London
W1N 7RJ
Tel: 0171 580 9360
Fax: 0171 637 1378
Publishes a wide range of books, pamphlets and reports on reproductive health including issues such as abortion, teenage pregnancy and sterilisation. A stamped, addressed envelope is required if seeking their publication list.

Department for International Development
94 Victoria Street
London
SW1E 5JL
Tel: 0171 917 0503
Fax: 0171 917 0021
Has a wide range of information about the British aid programme. Their annual review , *British Overseas Aid*, is available free at the above address.

Family Planning Association
2-12 Pentonville Road
London, N1 9FP
Tel: 0171 837 5432
Fax: 0171 837 3042
The FPA produces information and publications on all aspects of reproduction and sexual health – phone for a publications catalogue. Their Helpline (0171 837 4044 Monday-Friday 9am to 7pm) is run by qualified healthcare workers and can answer queries on all aspects of family planning.

International Planned Parenthood Federation (IPPF)
Regent's College
Inner Circle
Regent's Park
London, NW1 4NS
Tel: 0171 487 7900
Fax: 0171 487 7950
The world's largest voluntary organisation in the field of sexual and reproductive health, including family planning. They produce an extensive range of leaflets, books, posters and videos. Ask for their *Publications in Print* catalogue.

Marie Stopes International
153-157 Cleveland Street
London, W1P 5PG
Tel: 0171 574 7400
Fax: 0171 574 7417
Provides reproductive healthcare/ family planning services and information, to enable individuals all over the world to have children by choice, not by chance. Produces publications.

Oxfam
274 Banbury Road
Oxford
OX2 7DZ
Tel: 01865 311 311
Fax: 01865 313 770
Produces a wide range of publication including free leaflets. Ask for their Resources for Schools and Youth Workers catalogue.

Population Action International
1120 19th St., NW
Suite 550
Washington DC 20036
USA
Tel: 001 202 659 1833
Publishes the booklet *Why Population Matters*. Also publishes many other publications on the issue of population.

Population Concern
178-202 Great Portland Street
London, W1N 5TB
Tel: 0171 631 1546
Fax: 0171 436 2143
Population Concern, a charity, is currently working with local partners in 15 countries worldwide in South Asia, Africa, Latin America and the Caribbean to meet community demands for better healthcare and quality family planning. They produce a wide range of material including data sheets, maps, posters, factsheets, videos, student packs and a software pack on world population. Ask for their publications list.

Population Institute
107 Second Street
N.E. Washington DC 20002
USA
Tel: 001 202 544 3300
Publishes the magazine *Popline*.

Population Reference Bureau
1875 Connecticut Ave
NW Suite 520
Washington DC 20009-5728
USA
Fax: 001 202 328 3937

United Nations Population Fund (UNFPA)
220 East 42nd Street
New York NY10017
USA
Produces the magazine *Populi* which looks at reproductive health issues around the world.

INDEX

A
abortion
    deaths from 2, 14, 21
    and family planning programme 17, 39
    minimising the need for 38-9
    sex-selective 2, 27
    unsafe 2, 18, 21, 27
    and women's rights 32
adolescents *see* young people
Africa
    AIDS and population growth 5, 7
    birth rates 6, 26
    contraceptive use 25, 33
    family planning programmes 34, 35
      access to 36
    maternal mortality 4, 15
    population trends 1, 20
    teenage mothers 19, 20
    urban growth 10, 11, 12, 13
    women of child-bearing age 17
    young people 18
ageing population 7, 20
AIDS (Acquired Immune Deficiency
    Syndrome) 2, 5, 7, 18, 37
Asia
    access to contraception 33, 36
    bank loans for women 40
    birth rates 26
    contraceptive use 25
    maternal mortality 4
    population trends 16
    urban growth 10-11, 12, 13

B
biodiversity, loss of 8
birth rates
    in developing countries 6-7, 26
    falling 3, 7, 20, 35
    and family planning programmes 2, 36, 39
    outside marriage 35
    and population trends 5, 16
    and poverty 36
    in the United Kingdom 3
Brazil, family planning programme 2

C
Cairo Population Conference (1994) 2, 14, 15, 22, 32, 39
Caribbean
    access to contraception 33
    maternal mortality 4
    teenage mothers 20
    urban growth 10, 11, 13
Catholic Church, and contraception 14, 30
child mortality rates 36, 40
childless women 35
China
    birth rate 7
    family planning programmes 14, 15
coastal development, and population growth 9
condom use 33, 34, 38
consumption, and population growth 8-9, 15
contraceptives
    access by world region 33
    and the Catholic Church 14, 30
    reliability of 29
    use by world region 25
    see also family planning

D
deaths
    child mortality rates 36, 40
    from abortions 2, 14, 21
    from sexually transmitted diseases 2, 21
    maternal mortality 2, 4, 15, 17, 18, 19, 27
    and population trends 1, 3
developing countries
    birth rates 6-7, 26, 36
    factors in population control 1
    family planning programmes 6, 14, 17-18, 26, 39-40
      and men 34-5
    population growth 1, 4-5, 6-7, 14-15, 17
    population and poverty 36
    urban population 10
    young people in 17, 18

E
Earth carrying capacity 9
education, and female fertility rates 14, 20, 40
environment, and population growth 8-9, 14, 15
Europe
    ageing population 7, 20
    population trends 1, 5, 16
    urban population 10, 13

F
family planning
    developing countries 6, 14, 17-18, 26, 39-40
      and men 34-5
    and population growth 1, 5, 6, 14, 15, 17-18, 39-40
    rights of access to 24, 37
    and sexual and reproductive
      health 31-2
    spousal consent restrictions 34
    vasectomy 30-1
    see also contraceptives
fertility rates *see* birth rates

G
Ghana, family planning
programmes 35

42

global warming, and population growth 8

H
health care 27
HIV (Human Immuno-deficiency Virus) 2, 18, 21, 37, 38

I
India
    birth rates 5, 6
    family planning programmes 14
    pollution 15
    urban growth 12-13
Indonesia, family planning programmes 34-5
IPPF (International Planned Parenthood Federation),
    Charter on Sexual and Reproductive Rights 23
IUD (intra-uterine device) 33

J
Jordan, family planning programmes 35

L
land use, and population growth 9
Latin America
    abortions 14
    access to contraception 33
    bank loans for women 40
    birth rates 26, 40
    contraceptive use 25
    maternal mortality 4
    teenage mothers 18, 19, 20
    urban growth 10, 11, 12, 13
LEDCs (less economically developed countries) see
    developing countries
life expectancy
    in Africa 5
    in the UK 3

M
Malawi, family planning programmes 34, 35, 38
marriage, babies born outside 35
men
    contraceptive Pill for 28-30
    contraceptive use by world region 33
    and family planning programmes 34-5
    and vasectomy 30-1
Mexico, family planning programme 2
migration, and urban growth 12

N
Nigeria, family planning programme 2
Northern America
    urban growth 13

O
ozone depletion, and population growth 8

P
Philippines, family planning
programmes 2, 34
Pill, contraceptive
    access to by world region 33

for men 28-30
    and women in their 30s and 40s 33
pollution, and population growth 8
population control programmes 1-2, 39-40
    see also family planning
poverty 38
    and population 36
pregnancies
    maternal mortality 2, 4, 15, 17, 18, 19, 27
    teenage 18, 19-20, 25
    unwanted 2, 17, 18, 20, 21, 27

R
rape 2, 27
reproductive rights 21-5, 31-2
rights, reproductive 21-5, 31-2
Russia, environmental damage 8

S
STDs (sexually transmitted diseases) 2, 18, 21, 37

T
Third World see developing countries
tropical forests, and population growth 8-9

U
United States
    coastal development 9
    maternal mortality 4
    population growth 7
    teenage mothers 20
urban growth 10-13

V
vasectomy 30-1, 33
    in Malawi 34, 35

W
water resources, and population growth 9
women
    of child-bearing age 17, 39
    childless 35
    and the contraceptive Pill 33
    education for 14, 20, 40
    and genital mutilation 2, 22, 23, 27, 32
    numbers of children 3, 4, 6, 7, 14, 16, 18, 39
    and population growth 14
    and poverty 38
    and reproductive rights 21-5, 31-2, 37
    violence against 2, 22, 27, 32
    see also pregnancies
world population, growth rates 1, 6-7, 14-15, 16, 17-18

Y
young people 18, 19-20
    and the contraceptive Pill 33
    and reproductive rights 25, 37-8
    teenage pregnancies 18, 19-20, 25

ACKNOWLEDGEMENTS

The publisher is grateful for permission to reproduce the following material.

While every care has been taken to trace and acknowledge copyright, the publisher tenders its apology for any accidental infringement or where copyright has proved untraceable. The publisher would be pleased to come to a suitable arrangement in any such case with the rightful owner.

Chapter One: World Population

Focus on population, © Global Eye, Overseas Development Administration, Spring 1997, *The State of World Populations 1997*, © United Nations Population Fund, *Population to fall by 5m in 70 years*, © The Guardian, December 1996, *Population decline*, © Office for National Statistics, Crown Copyright 1997, *World population rises to 5·840 billion in 1997*, © Population Today, April 1997, *World population clock 1997*, © Population Reference Bureau, *World population growing more slowly than expected*, © The Guardian, November 1996, *Developing nations account for 98 percent of world population growth*, © Population Reference Bureau, *Average annual increase in world population*, © United Nations, *Population growth and consumption*, © Population Today, April 1997, *Urban population dynamics*, © UNFPA, January 1997, *The 30 largest countries ranked according to population size*, © United Nations, *Percentage of the population living in urban areas*, © United Nations, *Number of people living in urban areas*, © United Nations, *The processes of urban growth*, © UNFPA, *Urban growth by region*, © United Nations, *Harried by the mob*, © Times Newspapers Limited, February 1996, *Good news for 2050*, © People and the Planet, 1997, *What population problem?*, © The Alan Guttmacher Institute, *Population growth*, © USAID and US Bureau of the Census, *Young people and the world*, © UNFPA, *15m babies are born worldwide to adolescents each year*, © The Alan Guttmacher Institute, February 1997,

Scientists warn of ageing population next century, © The Guardian, June 1997.

Chapter Two: Family Planning

Reproductive neglect violates human rights, © Population Concern News, 1997, *Unplanned births*, © AGI, Hopes and Realities, *Several countries advancing women's rights*, © Popline, July/August 1997, *IPPF Charter on Sexual and Reproductive Rights*, © UNFPA, *Reproductive rights*, © United Nations, *Contraceptive use by region*, United Nations, *Family planning progress*, © Population Today, June 1997, *UNFPA stresses gender equality, maternal health*, © Popline, May/June 1997, *I'm the first man on the pill*, © Zest, June 1997, *Why Sandro has to keep taking the tablets*, © The Guardian, October 1997, *Pill for men blasted by Catholic groups*, © Catholic Herald, June 1997, *The truth about vasectomy*, © The Independent, June 1997, *The human right*, © International Planned Parenthood Federation, *Mothers in waiting*, © The Daily Mail, September 1996, *Access to contraception*, © United Nations, *Men take responsibility for reproductive health and family planning*, © UNFPA, *Childless women set to double*, © Telegraph Group Limited, London 1996, *Contraceptive preference*, © NOP, *Fact or fiction?*, © Actionaid, *Health and Choice and rights on the UK Government Agenda*, © Choices, 1997, *Today's choices – tomorrow's population*, © Population Action International.

Photographs and Illustrations

Pages 1, 12, 24: Michaela Bloomfield, pages 3, 14, 16, 31, 36: Ken Pyne, pages 6, 19, 23, 29, 32, 39: Andrew Smith, page 9: Katherine Fleming.

Craig Donnellan
Cambridge
January, 1998